"Bettie has an absolutely beautiful s̶t̶ ... g and intelligent. But what elevates her t̶o̶ ... ̶h her writing she has an indelible voice. ̶ ... re, it's special and it's simply a captivatin̶g̶ ...

... n Marx
... oducer

"Bettie Youngs has a talent for finding the essence of spirituality in various touching, and teaching, experiences. She opens her heart to life and, in so doing, opens our hearts to the beauty, depth and power of the human spirit. No one can read *Gifts of the Heart* without being moved—and improved."

Ruth Stafford Peale
cofounder and chair of the Peale Center for Christian Living

"Our daily actions have a great affect on those around us, whether or not we act in a conscious manner. In *Gifts of the Heart*, Bettie Youngs shows us how to ensure that what we share with others creates a positive effect. She gives us a roadmap for using the events of daily life to improve the world we live in and the lives of those with whom we share it."

John Bradshaw
New York Times bestselling author, *Bradshaw On: The Family* and *Homecoming*

"In almost everyone's life there occurs a turning point. For some it's a victory that brings new confidence, for others it's an unexpected defeat that makes them face themselves and the truth. As the stories in this excellent book show, it's not the event that redefines our lives so much as the way we handle it. You don't just read these stories with your eyes . . . you drink them with your heart and taste them with your soul. This book is a recipe for finding warmth, meaning and relevance."

Susan Ford Bales

"There are those times in life when our hearts have the opportunity to try something wiser—to choose another path. The stories show how to navigate the waters of life. A very special and very loving book."

John Gray
New York Times bestselling author, *Men Are from Mars, Women Are from Venus*

"I have always felt the importance of living and loving in the present. Bettie Youngs' loving book, *Gifts of the Heart*, reaffirms this for me. I couldn't put it down. I *loved* it!"

Florence Henderson
actress, singer

"Compassion, kindness, commitment and giving can open the heart. So can loneliness, grief, pain and duress. The stories in *Gifts of the Heart* illustrate with potent clarity the heart's ability to learn and grow, whether through challenges or joy, the ordinary or the extraordinary. A very loving book."

Richard Paul Evans
New York Times bestselling author, *The Christmas Box* and *Timepiece*

"Treasures . . . chocolates for the soul."

Sophy Burnham
journalist, playwright, *New York Times* bestselling author, *A Book of Angels*

"In this very beautiful book, Bettie illuminates the impact of one heart on another, allowing us to visit up close the delicate and fragile shifts that take place. These stories are about those magical and miraculous moments when tolerance, patience, grace, kindness, forgiveness and endurance are learned."

Harold Bloomfield, M.D.
New York Times bestselling author, *Making Peace with Yourself*

"The search for fulfillment is a human hunger that is much greater than humanistic unification and more powerful than political equality. It is a deep unrelenting search for spiritual reconciliation. As the stories in *Gifts of the Heart* sincerely show, spirit-led actions create life-changing, interdependent, affirming and accountable relationships—something to which we must all dedicate ourselves. As Bettie so eloquently says, 'It is the ultimate mission of the heart.'"

Bill McCartney
founder, The Promise Keepers

"In an age when many people are spending large quantities of time and energy for professional counseling, oft times we overlook an ever-present close friend and guide, the heart. Hearts are always available, day or night, at no cost. As Bettie Youngs relates in these warm and captivating stories, I have discovered the benefits of tuning into the heart. One can receive direction on matters ranging from the most complex to the simple. My favorite times in Habitat for Humanity are having the privilege of touching hearts by lending a helping hand: helping a family build a house, and then soon afterwards receive an even greater blessing on dedication day when the keys to a simple, decent house are presented along with a Bible to the family . . . gifts of the heart abound. But we can not leave these gifts locked up in a closet or even left unopened on a table. Thank you, Bettie, for sharing your 'opened' gift."

Linda Caldwell Fuller
cofounder, Habitat for Humanity International

of this exquisite book is that it's about real things, real people, real life. Some of the stories will make you laugh, others will make you cry. All will make you think. In real life we are often called upon to be responsible for others, sometimes when we don't always want to be. When we do this at the heart level, it becomes a choice, not a sacrifice. Real life (like real friendships) is pieced together from ordinary moments, many of which are humorous, sad, irritating and just plain work. All are meaningful in the scheme of things."

Caryl Kristensen and Marilyn Kentz
daytime ABC Television talk show hosts, *Caryl & Marilyn: Real Friends*

"Like Bettie, this book is pure magic. And I couldn't agree more when she says, 'One of the major tasks for which we are charged in our lifetimes, one of the dues we must pay for the privilege of our lives is to learn to love, to come from our hearts, to lead with our hearts.' It really is this simple: it's really the purpose of our lives. Please read this book today."

Wally "Famous" Amos
father of the chocolate chip cookie industry and inspirational
author, *Watermelon Magic: Seeds of Wisdom, Slices of Life*

"I love this book! It will wow your heart in a soul-penetrating way and expand your love, hope, helpfulness and encouragement towards others. Read it. Enjoy it. Give it to someone you love."

Mark Victor Hansen
author and editor, #1 *New York Times* bestselling series *Chicken Soup for the Soul*™

"To be able to speak to people's hearts—what a blessing, what an honor. Bettie has the ability to show us the world anew, to change the ways we think about ourselves and others. All of the love I've ever felt in my life is expressed in these stories: I laughed, cried, marveled, admired and learned. Such is the power of this glorious and touching book."

Barbara Billingsley
actress, Motion Picture Academy of Arts

"Find some still, quiet moments to linger over this book and feel your heart open a bit wider. Each story tenderly gives voice to the power of love and hope. Each story will help you reach out to those closest to you—or to complete strangers—with greater compassion."

Susan Skog
author, *Embracing Our Essence: Spiritual Conversations with Prominent Women*

"*Gifts of the Heart* reveals and nurtures the most precious and powerful of human experiences: the ability to grow through love and being loved."

Denis Waitley, Ph.D.
New York Times bestselling author, *Empires of the Mind*

"Bettie's last book, *Values from the Heartland,* is one of the very finest books I've ever read. Now she gives us another beautiful book, one filled with stories that could well be received as if a basket of gifts, each one packaged in day-to-day life, tied with the bows of vivid detail, unwrapping to reveal a precious token of deep human truth. Like healthy food nourishes and sustains the body, *Gifts of the Heart* will nourish and sustain your heart and soul."

Jenny Craig
founder and vice chair of *Jenny Craig International*

"Bettie has uncovered the personal style found deep within our hearts. Through stories rich in detail, the interior of our lives becomes the exterior. These moving stories expose the human heart's tryst with understanding, compassion and its ability to unfold untold measures of love."

Barbara Hiser
Emmy Award-winning producer, *Caroline in the City*

"Once more, with love. Oustanding."

Kim Peak
the real-life inspiration for *Rain Man*

"The real art of magic is that it forces people to think. Bettie's methods of adjusting the visceral perspective force us to not only think, but to feel, care and appreciate life from many perspectives. In *Gifts of the Heart* she seduces your emotions with the finesse of the most adroit conjurer."

Brian Gillis
world-class magician, Academy of Magical Arts,
VIP Sleight-of-Hand Entertainer for the 1996 Olympics

"Bettie Youngs is a compassionate, articulate, loving, inspirational and insightful purveyor of the overlooked. She simply sees things most of us don't. These stories are truly *Gifts of the Heart*. To know this book is to know giving. To know giving is to know love. Being truly loved can change the way we look at ourselves, and the world around us."

Graham Ledger
two-time Emmy Award-winning anchor, Channel 8, NBC Television

"Most of us never figure people out. Instead, we ricochet through life getting along with some people, refusing to deal with others, and having very little inter-action with still others because they are so different from us. As the stories in this marvelous book show, we can learn to communicate with people more effec-tively if we listen from the heart."

Tony Alessandra, Ph.D.
author, *The Platinum Rule*

"Make the choice to acknowledge the best in yourself and the world around you will change. This magnificent book good for your heart. Give it to others is, and it'll be good for theirs. Good hearts make a real and lasting difference in the world."

Dottie Walters
founder and president, Walters International Speakers Bureau

"When I spoke at my father's funeral, I asked all present to cherish and celebrate what he gave us, not mourn what we lost. Today I read *Gifts of the Heart* and cried. These joyful tears helped me recall the gifts Dad and others have given me over the years. People who read this book will become better people. Bettie Youngs has given us a gift that will cause us to be better parents, better friends, better workers and better neighbors."

Jim Cathcart
past president, National Speakers Association and author, *The Acorn Principle*

"With insight and caring compassion, Bettie Youngs illuminates the courage and passion required to love life with all your heart. This book is a feast for the heart. Its stories savor the substance of love."

Arthur Samuel Joseph
author, *The Sound of the Soul*

"Ghandi reminded us that some mountains can only be moved by prayer. This exceptionally poignant book reminds us that some of those mountains exist in our heads, and shows us how the heart moves mountains—exceptionally relevant as we strive to make our homes, communities and the world a better place in which to live. This loving book beckons us to rise above repressed thinking and encour-ages us to lead with our hearts."

Brian Klemmer
founder, Personal Mastery Seminars

"Bettie Youngs has once again shown us that true happiness (and satisfaction with one's life) is a result of long-term investments of time and emotions in the things we love and value. In these beautiful short stories, Bettie shares what these investments are and subtly challenges us to take stock. In this marvelous book she gives us an inventory check-off sheet for the heart."

Ron Giancola
director of pupil personnel services, Sewanhaka Central High School District, NY

Gifts of the Heart

STORIES THAT CELEBRATE LIFE'S DEFINING MOMENTS

Bettie B. Youngs, Ph.D., Ed.D.

Health Communications, Inc.
Deerfield Beach, Florida

Library of Congress Cataloging-in-Publication Data

Youngs, Bettie B.
    Gifts of the heart: stories that celebrate life's defining moments/Bettie
    B. Youngs.
            p.   cm.
        ISBN 1-55874-419-3
        1. Youngs, Bettie B.—Anecdotes.   2. Human behavior—Anecdotes.   I.
    Title.
CT275.Y65A3   1996
150'.92—dc20   96-9782
[B]   CIP

Publisher: Health Communications, Inc.
            3201 S.W. 15th Street
            Deerfield Beach, Florida 33442-8190

Cover illustration and design by Andrea Perrine Brower

*It's not the great things you do
that matter, but the small things you
do with great heart.*

—Mother Teresa

*Someday, after we have
mastered the winds, the waves,
the tides and gravity, we shall harness the
energies of love. Then, for the second time
in the history of the world, man will
have discovered fire.*

—Teilhard de Chardin

The Mother Teresas of the world exist everywhere: in our homes, in our work places, in our communities. We need only to open our own hearts to recognize and appreciate their—and our—extraordinary contributions to ordinary moments. This book is dedicated to all those who offer us the gifts of their hearts; their loving actions harness the energies of passion, compassion and integrity, and confirm that love really is the most potent and transforming force in all the world.

Also by Bettie B. Youngs

Contents

Acknowledgments

Launching a book can be like watching an ant colony: the multitude of tasks to be done and the number of those intricately at work are staggering. To the family at Health Communications, Inc.: publishers Peter Vegso and Gary Seidler for their belief and support in my work; for the sensitive editing of Matthew Diener, Christine Belleris and Erica Orloff; Kim Weiss and Randee Goldsmith in publicity; and to the many other members of the team it is with respect and admiration that I offer a heartfelt thanks for their collective efforts on birthing this book.

As a writer I notice book covers. Let's face it, most are ho-hum. This is not the case with the beautiful design of this book, *Gifts of the Heart,* and my previous book, *Values from the Heartland.* Both were designed by Andrea Perrine Brower. Thank you Andrea for seeing the spirit within these two books and for the translation into radiant covers.

My work over the years has taken me to every corner of the globe, and then some. The diversity of people I've encountered along the way has been an education in its own right. But even more impressive has been the sense of kinship along the way, expanding my ability to love and be loved. As a result, I no longer feel like I live in any particular city or state, but rather the worldplace. Thank you to the many of you who share yourselves with me in so many selfless ways and teach me a richer meaning of being a fellow traveler. Firsthand I have learned that though there is much dissonance in the world, there is equally as much peace, kindness and loving people. It helps to keep in mind that we are all soul-journers.

To the many many friends who stay connected and offer friendship and support, I offer a heartfelt thanks, as I do to my family, especially my parents and brothers and sisters. Your unconditional love, support and encouragement over the years is an anchor offering untold sustenance. Being a part of this large, loving and loyal family has been a gift for which I am enormously appreciative.

And lastly, for the incompressible joy of being her mom, and for her unwavering courage to live her truths, I acknowledge my dear daughter, Jennifer. She shares my heart and soul in oh so many ways.

Introduction

The Amazing Human Heart

Throughout the ages, in almost every known culture and faith, the word "heart" has been used to describe the cradle of our feelings; sometimes, even the birth of them. But of course it is more. The human heart is the primary organ of our circulatory system; each of us is dependent upon it to keep one's life's blood pumping. Medically, as long as a person's heart still beats, she is considered alive. Being the center of the circulation of each individual's life, the heart is designated as the home that harbors and protects not only our very life force, but the core of our emotional vivacity and capacity for feelings. This makes it worthy to represent and become symbolic for the most priceless gift of all—love. The universal symbol for the heart is love and, in turn, the symbol for love is the shape of a heart.

How appropriate. The very symbol of a heart conjures up feelings of tenderness, of affection, of caretaking. What greater force for good, what greater depth of emotion, what greater power for growth and healing of the whole being exists in our world today?

The duality of the physical and emotional is certainly not just a modern-day notion. There are records as far back as 825 A.D. which refer to *heorte* as both a physical organ and the seat of emotions.

The metaphor "heart" seems apropos when we explore the literal definitions. In every dictionary, anatomical definitions lead to those such as "the vital center of one's being, emotions and sensibilities; the repository of one's sincerest feelings and beliefs." We don't have to search far to discover how the emotional and physical aspects of these meanings have been integrated—we put our hand over our heart when we stand at attention during the Pledge of Allegiance; we wear a wedding ring on what we refer to as the "ring finger," which was thought to have a vein that went to the heart and thus became the "romance finger."

The word "heart" as we know it today originated from the Old English word *heorte,* having first evolved from the Middle English word *hert.* This simple, one syllable, five-letter word—a core word of the English language—has many connotations: courage, stamina, generosity, charity and kindness are all dictionary synonyms of heart. A complete list of commonly used idioms illustrating the multiple meanings of heart used in everyday language proves seemingly endless.

The following one, though only partial, gives us some idea of its vastness:

- a broken heart—great disappointment or sorrow.
- speaking from the heart—to honestly express one's deepest feelings and beliefs.
- at heart—basically, in reality, fundamentally.
- by heart—to remember exactly, word for word.
- heart knowledge—to know through experience at a level deeper than intellect.

- from the bottom of one's heart—with complete sincerity.
- in one's heart of hearts—deep within one's self.
- set one's heart on—wish for intensely; pursue with determination.
- have one's heart in the right place—to have good intentions; to be basically kind.
- near one's heart—of great interest or concern to one.
- take heart—to regain courage or strength.
- with all one's heart—with earnestness or enthusiasm.
- have a heart—to be compassionate or merciful.
- eat one's heart out—to have envy, longing or sorrow dominate one's emotions; grieve inconsolably.
- wear one's heart on one's sleeve—to allow one's intimate feelings or personal affairs to be known to everyone.
- cross one's heart—to maintain the truth of a statement; affirm one's integrity.
- to one's heart's content—until one is satisfied.
- do someone's heart good—to give happiness or pleasure to.
- take or lay to heart—to seriously consider and think about.
- have at heart—to have as an object, aim or desire.
- have one's heart in one's mouth—to be very anxious or fearful.
- set one's heart at rest—to dismiss one's anxieties.
- not have the heart—to lack the necessary courage to do something.

- heart and soul—fervently; completely; enthusiastically.
- lose one's heart—to fall in love with.

Were we to explore each definition, we'd be one step closer to grasping the expansive significance of "heart." In fact, some dictionaries dedicate almost five complete pages to this simple word, its origin and history.

Integrating all definitions past and present, heart can be evidenced in observing how we humans deal with our lives, particularly in coping with the stress, strains and obstacles we are sure to encounter. It's this evidence that clarifies the essence of our heart; a marathon runner who overcomes all physical limitations and completes a race; an impoverished person who rises above his or her environment and achieves meaning, purpose and success; a parent who unconditionally loves and stands by her children in all their encounters; the person who endures when faced with personal devastation; a child who flourishes even when parental love and caretaking is limited or hurtful.

Think of all we ask of our hearts, from appreciating the intricate beauty of a fragile butterfly, bonding with and forever protecting a wrinkle-faced newborn, triumphing or overcoming tragedy, to healing from loss and relishing joy and love. Regardless of the nature of the task—whether large or small—we ask our hearts to sift through it, to savor the experience lovingly, in ways that offer an even deeper understanding, appreciation and acceptance of life. In joy, pain or devastation, we ask our hearts to "go on." Such is the case in the true story below in which a mother finds the will to love and raise her remaining family after losing two children and her husband in a tragic automobile accident.

In her last moments of consciousness, Elaine remembered hearing a loud popping noise, immediately followed by the terrifying sound of shattering glass and metal crushing in all around her, and the sensation of tumbling. Then chilling silence screamed out in the darkness. Her eyes adjusted to the dim light of night and she regained vision just in time to exchange glances with her beloved husband John as he drew his last breath and slipped away.

He was the love of her life. For 21 years they were bound together in a loving partnership, one they each fondly referred to as their "soulship." They had settled in Northern California and, as he so aptly put it, "started a business and a 'nest'—together." Their "flock" consisted of their eldest child—a daughter, now 20—and not one, but two sets of twins—two boys, now 16, and a boy and a girl, 13.

In some families members tolerate and "put up" with each other. This family was different: its members genuinely liked and honored each other.

The wedding of their oldest daughter was the reason for the trip to Southern California. Their daughter had met her future husband while attending college in the Los Angeles area. The ceremony was being held not far from campus during a holiday break. Looking forward to the opportunity to have the entire family together for an important event, the proud parents and siblings of the bride-to-be packed up and departed on the journey south. The plan was to leave immediately after the soccer game of the youngest children and travel the distance while the four children slept in the back of the eight-passenger minivan.

Stopping in the emergency lane, Elaine changed from passenger to driver, offering her husband some much-needed rest. While accelerating into the early morning flow of freeway traffic she heard a loud pop, later explained as the steering mechanism failing. Suddenly the minivan and its precious cargo veered into the path of a passing 18-wheeler semi-truck. In the blink of an eye, their lives changed forever.

When she awoke in the intensive care unit, a doctor told her what she already knew in her heart: not only had her dear husband been taken, but also one of each set of twins. She was then apprised of her own condition—two badly crushed legs and the serious bruising of vital organs. The two remaining twins, both seriously injured, were expected to recover.

As the impact of the words slowly took on their full meaning, she felt the gripping, stabbing pain of her heart breaking. How could she go on? Where would she get the strength and courage to help her young children heal *all* their wounds? How could she be on friendly terms with life now? What could possibly bring joy to her life after such a loss?

Her request to have herself and her children moved into the same hospital room so they could all be comforted and strengthened by being together was granted. The doctors, nurses and hospital staff were overwhelmed to see the physically and emotionally devastated remains—now all in the same room—of a once whole and vibrant family unit. Each family member was a critical case, each was grieving extreme loss and each was trying to find the inner strength and will for the fight to survive, recover and find meaning.

"How will you go on?" friends and family asked.

"We'll find a way," she said. "We'll search our hearts and find a way."

Late one night, she awoke to the uncontrollable weeping of her younger son who, through his tears, sobbed, "I want to see my sister, my brother and my dad; where are they? Why . . . Why did this happen? It can't . . . they didn't . . . NO!" Her young son's profound and immeasurable pain seared her already broken heart and blasted open yet another dam of tears. It is such a secret place, the land of tears. She had wept so much already, she was sure all her body's fluids must be depleted by now and wondered where the tears could come from. "Be strong, be strong," she counseled herself, knowing that like the protagonist in Margaret Rose Powers' "Footprints," she needed not only to be cared for, but carried. In that poignant prose, God promises to lift the burden and provide needed respite at the very lowest and saddest times in a Christian's life. And so she turned to what she knew to be the supreme root of all strength and prayed: "Please God, help me. And help me help these children of mine; what should I say, what should I do?"

Before she could comfort her grieving son, his older brother reached out to soothe him. "I know you miss them, so do I, Bro," he said gently through tears of his own. "But they haven't left us, Brian. My twin is right here beside me, I can see him and I can feel him. Feel our brother and sister and Dad, Brian. They're all here. If you can't see them, feel them with your heart." He put one hand over his own heart, and with the other, lovingly reached out through the darkness to touch his brother's hand in the hospital bed next to his. For added reassurance he said once again, "Even if we can't see them with our eyes, they're here." He paused then, and without a single trace of uncertainty, applied the ultimate balm to his brother's deep wounds. "Brian, now we each have our own angel watching out for us . . . for the rest of our lives. You'll have your twin sister, I have my twin brother and Mom has Dad. They're all right here with us and they're going to be with us always, in all times. Forever."

Hearing this touching scene between her sons helped their mother know that they would be all right. It was a matter of time and healing. But more, her son's words of insight offered comfort for her as well. She closed her eyes feeling her family, too—all of them—and knew that not only must she go on, but that she could and that she would muster the strength to lead the way.

The next morning all members of this family were different. They were more at peace, more resolved. And more. Their strength and resiliency had doubled.

Healing, in all forms, began anew.

The following days and weeks of recovery were long and agonizing for each of them, yet together they found the strength and the heart to go on.

The heart to go on? Is it the heart that leads the journey? Is the heart the kernel, core or fruit of our motivation? Is it all of these, serving in all roles?

Just what is this intangible power of the heart, this emotional endowment that can be so enormously felt yet is so difficult to name? Is it a force—ours for the asking—that can give wings to seemingly impossible feats and deeds? Is it an ability that allows us not only to recover from defeats and tragedies, but in doing so, to possess an even greater capacity for compassion, courage, insight, sincerity, charity, kindness and generosity? How is it that the heart, in the wake of a traumatic experience—one as tragic as the family shattered at the hands of death—causes and allows the human spirit to emerge with a greater sense of stamina, perseverance, determination, resilience and enthusiasm— all positive strengths of character—instead of being incapacitated, withering under the strain of negative feelings such as anger, bitterness, hatred and loss?

However it happens, it can be so; sometimes a flower gives off its most luscious fragrance after it has been crushed. Likewise, as each of us asks our heart for the courage to go on, we find it ready to be of service. In fact, as we ask our hearts to help us endure the bruises and abrasions of life—as we go about our journey up and over the hills, across the seas and around the mountains—it does more than make the trip, it perseveres and expands its capacity to generate understanding and love. What a miraculous outcome.

Almost without exception, we are told that love is the most potent force in all the world. Almost without exception, we are told that our earthly mission is to expand our capacity to love along the way.

Could our life's work be to discover, develop and then care for the strengths our hearts uncover as we go about our lives? Could the task be to fill our hearts like quivers with the attributes that enable us to overcome and triumph over the personal adversities we face in life? I think so. I think it is one of the major tasks for which we are charged in our lifetimes. One of the dues we must pay for the privilege of our lives is to learn to love—to come from our hearts, to lead with our hearts.

Acknowledging the heart's magical and magnificent ability to ignite within us a powerful torch—the brightness of which is often outside our realm of understanding, yet its presence and effect in our lives is undeniable—is perhaps the greatest tool we have to live out the purpose of our lives, to make the time we are given count for something, to matter. Such is the mission of the heart.

We are each in search of our own life quests, each experiencing our own lives. We are each our own hero. May we be guided by our hearts.

My last book, *Values from the Heartland*—a collection of heartwarming short stories exploring the deeper side of integrity, commitment, honor, self-discipline, connection and character—illustrates values in action. It illuminates how values, principles and other worthy ideals are assimilated in the daily exchange between people—family members, friends, colleagues, members of an interdependent community—moments where we reveal our finest qualities. I wrote *Values from the Heartland* because it is my sincere belief that people learn about goodness and compassion when they see it, feel and hear of it in action. We see, feel and hear so much negativity, hurt and violence: we are more in need of positive models than critics. Luckily, there is no shortage of them. What is enriching and lasting in life is the result of long-term investments in the people we love and care about. My goal in writing the book was to inspire us to not only remember these everyday heroes and their willingness to show us the way, but to recognize that it was often the richness and vibrancy of their very nature that inspired us to assimilate worthy goals and ideals. Often these crucial lessons are passed on to us in subtle moments without fanfare, in what I am fond of referring to as "teachable moments." These moments ring too loud for the heart not to hear. Goodness and kindness are powerful wings on which such lessons alight in our hearts.

Teachable moments seem to have one feature in common: they are products of the heart. As Antoine de Saint Exupéry's classic fable, *The Little Prince,* teaches, "it is only with the heart that one can see rightly."

As someone who has worked with people in "teachable moments" for nearly 25 years now, I know the importance of the heart being at work if our vision is to be clear; if our mission is to be guided by real truths and if needed change is to be lasting. In *Gifts of the Heart,* my goal is to illustrate and celebrate with true experiences the human heart's ability to discover, transform and expand its capacity to love, so that it may see rightly. Such "sight" comes in those defining moments when the heart is open. Those moments can be immediate or they can be a long time in arriving.

Whether gained through facing everyday challenges, or from joy, pain and healing, many of the experiences in our lives trigger an opportunity for the heart to gain a deeper understanding, appreciation and acceptance of life—and of others. Tolerance, patience, grace, kindness and forgiveness can be the result.

The stories in this book highlight the process and the action of that core of emotion, that soul or essence of being, that spirit of life within each of us as it learns, grows and responds. In this book, I have called these experiences "defining moments."

Examples of the heart at work are all around us. As the diversity of these stories shows, they happen everywhere, in every facet of life, to people of all ages and walks of life. Whether on the wings of a child, co-worker, angel or pet, the potency of a lesson learned from a heart at work is touching and eloquent. Its down-to-earth revelations of the deeper workings of our emotions help us reclaim our personal truths. May we use these as a springboard to expand our capacity to be responsive and loving—both to ourselves and our fellow travelers—in our homeplace, workplace and worldplace.

Observing others who face special challenges and respond from their heart, are "true" to their hearts, can give our hearts cause to reflect. This can be a needed transfusion, triggering inspiration and growth, and revealing truth. The Greek word for truth, *althea*, doesn't mean the opposite of falsehood; rather it means the opposite of oblivion: The truth is what is remembered. May the stories in this book instill a deeper integration of truth in our hearts by helping us remember how that truth exists for each of us personally. And lastly, may we each give and receive the gifts of the heart.

1

The Two
Old People

*Our true destiny is not to be ministered
unto but to minister to ourselves
and to our fellow men.*

—Franklin Delano Roosevelt

They were inseparable. When he went for a morning walk she tagged along, harassing him about this or that, moaning, groaning and complaining bitterly all the way. She preferred to walk in the evening. When she went for her evening walk, he went along grudgingly, invited or not, badgering her about this or that, moaning, groaning and complaining bitterly all the way.

Everyone called them "the two old people." They squabbled about this and squabbled about that. Then they squabbled some more. They bickered about more than the time of day each preferred to go for his or her daily walk. Anything and everything was fodder for a quarrel. If they weren't battling each other, they would feud with someone else, and then argue about it between themselves later.

Unfortunately, they lived in the condominium above mine. Living in such close confines—and in a warm and sunny climate that allows for doors and windows to be kept open much of the time—meant I was often privy to what I referred to as their "willful emotional abuse" of each other.

I had my share of run-ins with them as well. If the evening breeze lifted the smoke from the barbecue grill on my patio and carried it high into the air, they accused me of deliberately trying to smoke them out of their home. If the breeze carried the smoke somewhere other than their direction, then it was the rich aromas from the chicken or juicy steaks I basted in delicious herbs and spices that all too "intensely invaded" their little haven in the sky. Every time their nostrils detected these "repugnant odors"—which was just about every time I used my grill—the two old people alleged that the "smells" interfered with their sinuses and caused them breathing difficulties.

Innocent children fared no better than the meat on my grill. When my neighbor's little girl swam in the children's pool and gleefully laughed as she splashed water on her playmate, they labeled these life-affirming sounds an "annoying disturbance." According to the pair, it caused afternoon insomnia and a loss of their right to the peace they deserved in their golden years.

No one was exempt, not even the tennis players in the far-off distance at the local courts. The nic, knock, nic, knock sound of fluffy tennis balls bouncing from one side of the court to the other resulted in the two old people writing a scathing letter to the condominium board. They claimed the "awful ruckus of the thudding balls" bombarded their sensitive ears with an "intrusive and obnoxious sound," causing the old man's hearing aid to malfunction.

We all thought they were miserable people.

One evening as I prepared to turn in, I made the usual round of locking doors, turning out the lights and checking in on my daughter. This included making sure her two kittens were accounted for. My daughter was asleep in her bed. In the kittens' basket beside her bed slept Otis, the docile, little gray male kitten, but his feisty, little orange-colored sister, Pumpkin, was not beside him. Usually where one went, the other followed. Either two kittens curled up with each other in their basket, or both jumped onto my daughter's bed and snuggled around the breathing sounds of their mistress. Often I tucked my Jennifer into bed, kissed her goodnight and, as I left the room, observed the two little bodies of long-haired kittens huddled together in their basket, each kitten peering at me with one drowsy eye keeping a watchful account of my actions while the other eye remained closed and asleep. More often than not, by morning those same kitties lay asleep in my daughter's bed, usually nestled in her long hair or with their little noses pressed against my seven-year-old's neck. Sometimes the kittens were fast asleep with their little heads resting on my daughter's muscular little arms; they especially enjoyed the wrist area and the crooks of her elbows. Every now and then I found Jennie asleep on the floor near her kittens, her blanket pulled to the floor with her. Against the advice of her pediatrician, I had given up separating this little girl of mine from her cats. If they didn't sleep with her, she slept with them.

On this night, Pumpkin was neither in her own bed, nor under or in my daughter's. I searched the house over: Pumpkin was nowhere to be found. Perhaps, I thought, we had inadvertently locked the little cat outside. I took the flashlight and searched outside our home—still no Pumpkin. I decided to walk down the well-lit path leading to the central park of the condominium complex. It was here that my daughter took the kittens to play after school each day, so I knew they were familiar with the spot. Late on this exceptionally still evening, crickets, birds and other creatures of the night chorused a rich array of songs, their melodies somehow more striking muted by the background sounds of the city. My senses strained to adjust to this night's environment, sharpening their abilities to interpret the myriad energies around me. I stopped, turned off the flashlight and listened. Hearing a kitten's faint cry that I was pretty sure belonged to Pumpkin, I clicked on the light and shined it in the direction of the sound up into a nearby sapling. There was Pumpkin all right, her plump little body supported only by a frail branch, the narrow limb dividing her round little belly equally into two halves. Any move the kitten made caused her hind legs to slip off the branch and dangle in mid-air; frantically, she pedaled her legs in an attempt to regain her grasp of the branch. It was a futile effort. Meanwhile, her two front paws clung desperately to the slender limb of the young tree. Combined, these actions made the branch gently sway up and down from her weight. Pumpkin was too frightened to retrace the steps she had taken to get there in the first place. When the panic-stricken kitten saw me, her whimpering instantly transformed into shrill almost angry meows that both begged for help and feared her rescuer.

Pumpkin and I had a relationship of tolerance. Pumpkin tolerated me, especially if my hand held or carried food and my feet were heading in the direction of her feeding dish. I tolerated Pumpkin living in the house, especially if she obeyed the rules of never sitting on the furniture. Unlike our alliance, the relationship between Jennifer and Pumpkin was unconditional. They were two of a kind: funny, sassy, loving, playful, adventurous.

Pumpkin was the first kitten born to the stray cat that visited the patio of our home every day even though she didn't belong to us. And when the stray decided to give birth to her kittens, it was our patio she chose. As was the stray's luck—or good instincts—Jennie took her in. As expected, my Jennie—the Mother Teresa of the cat kingdom—not only took her in, but gave her a birthing bed in the corner of her closet. There among well-used soccer shoes, a worn-out baseball glove signed by her friends, buddies and teammates over the years, two baseball bats, an odd assortment of hoarded tennis balls retrieved from the nearby courts, crumpled papers of long-lost homework assignments, and a dead or near-dead bug collection in jars capped with lids frequently stabbed and jabbed, the mother cat promptly delivered two kittens. When the mother cat nursed her two kittens for as long as they needed—or for as long as she wanted to, whether the kittens were ready to be weaned or not—she reclaimed her independence as easily as she had given it up when she needed caretaking. Without thinking twice—or perhaps after a great deal of thought— she left her two kittens in Jennifer's care.

Of the two kittens, Pumpkin was my daughter's favorite. Kitten and child played together and put up with each other's antics. Pumpkin submitted to being dressed in cut-up socks, to having her hair combed, barretted and hair sprayed. Whether the kitten liked it or not, when cartoons were on, sitting on Jennie's lap was mandatory. Sometimes the kitten would lie in Jen's lap of her own volition, at other times she stayed in place by brute force (Jennie's). Against my wishes, Pumpkin often lapped milk from Jennie's cereal bowl and consumed other human food as well. Though only seven man-months old, perhaps the kitten had already used up several of her legendary nine lives as a playmate of my tomboy daughter. If she did, it was, no doubt, a good trade. Kitten and child belonged together.

Compassion, sympathy and stepchild member of the family aside, the spectacle of the scared little cat clutching the tiny tree branch and holding on for dear life was hilarious.

Here was Pumpkin, her long, silky orange-colored hair now soaking wet from the night's dew on the tree leaves, disheveled in a most fascinating spike-like fashion, with a wide-eyed look of startled terror in her pale blue eyes. The nostrils of the tiny, pink button nose on her little round face now heaved a mile a minute as they responded to her body's need for an increased supply of oxygen due to her intense stress. The tiny delicate mouth that housed a dainty pink tongue and sharp little teeth was now wide open and emitting frantic, high-pitched meows between hissing sounds.

"Pumpkin," I said, laughing, "you look pathetic! I'd give up being hostile if I were you. This is a good time to be humble and grateful. You're in quite a predicament, and you look like you need help. Now, I'll help you down if you promise to stop sleeping on my couch when I'm at work!" Responding to the familiarity of my voice, the little cat meowed softly. Coming from the feisty kitten, this feeble sound with its note of plea tugged at my heart. All teasing forgotten, I felt for her. "Okay, come here, you poor little thing! I'll help you, no strings attached."

I turned the flashlight off, laid it on the ground and climbed up into the base of the tree. I reached up into the leaves to lift the kitty to safety. Grabbing her with one hand around her little body, I could feel her heart beating frantically, probably as much from her apprehension of my reaching for her as from her anxiety at being helplessly stranded. Frightened—and always more loyal to my daughter than to me—she hissed and clawed. I quickly tucked her into my sweatshirt. I pulled it snug around her and stroked her in an attempt to calm her and control her desire to get away.

Climbing down the spindly tree with one hand while the other held the kitten in place would be tricky. I sat for a moment to ponder my dilemma. It was then that I heard sharp voices approaching. I sat motionless and listened intently, trying to decipher whose voices I heard.

"If you hadn't . . ." a woman's shrill voice accused scornfully.

"It wasn't *me*," a male voice interrupted with an angry shriek. "She would still be alive if . . ."

The woman broke into his angry tone with one of her own and tried to finish his sentence for him. "If *you* had been a better father, one who . . ."

He interrupted her interruption. "And *you*?" he railed in a harsh, sarcastic tone. "Were *you* such a great mother?" His voice held tears, also.

With as much hurt as anger, the woman wailed, "She was my daughter! Paula. Oh, my Paula." She sobbed uncontrollably.

"We still have Robby. He's a good son," the old man countered softly. There was untold pain in his voice. "We . . . have . . . Robby."

Paying no heed to the late night jogger who approached and then passed them, the old woman cried aloud, "Robert is not my daughter. No one can replace my Paula."

"It was a tragic accident," the old man offered. "It was. It was . . ." He stopped in mid-sentence as though in that moment he, too, recognized that the depth of his loss was without bottom. His short, stocky body shuddered with a sigh. I watched as the light-colored fishing cap he always wore moved slowly back and forth. He shook his head and softly said, "It was so many years ago. You must come to terms with her death. We must forgive ourselves."

"*Never!*" she screeched.

The voices belonged to the two old people. They strolled out of sight, taking their hurt with them.

Hearing this troubling exchange made me feel uneasy, leaving within me a feeling of great anxiety. It was more than this couple's hostility, anger and blaming each other that was disturbing. Apparently there had been a great tragedy in their lives: They had lost a child. I couldn't fathom what it would be like to lose one's child. How does a parent regain equilibrium? How does she refill the enormity of such a loss? My thoughts turned to my precious daughter asleep in her bed. I hurried home.

That little Pumpkin was one mischievous kitten. Nearly a year old, she was a veteran scout, no longer intimidated by a fragile branch swaying in the breeze—especially if nestled in its leaves was a nest. Without one bit of hesitation, Pumpkin would help herself to birds' eggs and, on occasion, a bird, too. Nor was it beneath her dignity to stalk the beautiful birds singing and chirping as they innocently bathed in the waterfalls located throughout the lush grounds of the condominium complex, or to tease and playfully terrorize the little green garden lizards scampering in the underbrush. Field mice darting from one space to the next often fell prey to the gigantic orange monster with paws as quick as a mousetrap. No potential delicacy was safe from her well-executed, furry pounce and capture.

When the six acres of garden grounds no longer satisfied Pumpkin's insatiable curiosity for exploration, she took to crossing the street and raiding the neighbors' yards as well.

One day Pumpkin met a car that didn't see a little orange-colored cat out on a prowl for a picnic.

We found Pumpkin late that afternoon, her limp body lying lifeless by the side of the street near our complex.

It's difficult to help a young child understand her pet's death. The simple explanation of a two-ton car meeting up with a two-pound skeleton covered with fluffy hair does not suffice. My daughter carried her cat back to the house, crying the entire way. Though mortified that someone could hit the cat without notifying its owner, she could find no words to express her feelings.

Jennie wasn't ready to accept her cat's death. I knew she needed time and allowed this to her. Helping my daughter deal with the death of *her* pet was a new experience for me, too. I was grateful for the time to find a way to put the intangibility of "death" into peanut-butter-and-jelly language. Dinner was an hour away; I would wait until then to talk over the cat's death and our intentions for its burial.

The dinner hour arrived and I went to Jennie's room to get her. She wasn't there—nor was she on the patio. Not only was my daughter not there, the cat's corpse wasn't there either. I went looking. The park seemed the place to begin. Perhaps she had gone there to mourn—or perhaps she had decided to bury her precious little pet on her own.

As I neared the park, I was surprised by what I saw before me. I stopped to take it all in. There on the wooden park bench sat my almost-eight-year-old daughter, cradling in her arms the large blue bath towel in which we had wrapped the dead cat. How I loved this child of mine. Instantly, I felt her pain searing into my heart and wept for her innocence lost. She sat cross-legged on the bench, still dressed in her Little–League softball uniform, white trousers with blue stripes up the sides and permanent grass stains that would never come out, regardless of promises made by the television commercials. Sewn in bold letters on her white jersey was her favorite number, 12. It was "her number," she considered it her lucky charm. Her school locker was #12, as was just about everything that needed a number assigned to it. She had etched this number on the laminated covers of her school notebooks and writing pads and anything else that needed decoration. Born under the zodiac's 12th sign—Pisces—its oldest and wisest child, a sign of compassion and enlightenment, the intuitive, in tune with the synchronicities of the universe, the sign of the healer, Jennie possessed all the duplicity of the twin fishes, both a teacher and yet the most vulnerable.

Number 12 sat with her white Cubs baseball cap with its royal blue bill pulled down to shadow her tear-filled eyes. I was just about to go to her when the old woman carrying pots of soil approached the bench where Jen sat. It wasn't uncommon to see the woman pulling weeds in the park's garden or gathering up soil to take to her patio, for one of the many potted plants she regularly tended.

As the old woman approached the bench, her weary stride slowed. She'd obviously been looking for a place to rest and was now grudgingly concerned with the young girl grieving on the bench she'd selected for her respite. Her eyes going to the towel Jennie cradled, the old woman sat down carefully, then in the same manner set down the pots she held and a small spade with clumps of moist soil still clinging to it. Clearing her throat, her plump body scooted cautiously towards Jen as she inquired, "So, what is it you have there?" There was something rusty about her attempt to comfort, as if her heart wouldn't quite cooperate. In her pain, Jennie was beyond deciphering inflections and sobbed, "My kitty, Pumpkin—she's dead."

The old woman huddled closer to the child, and the two exchanged murmured words. In and of itself this was an interesting sight, the senior was such a standoffish sort of person and had a reputation for her disdain of children, especially active busybodies like my daughter. But now she sat with the child, her body language every bit intertwined with the little girl. The wrinkles on her round face furrowed further as she pulled her white eyebrows together, puckered her lips and clucked in distressed sympathy. She placed one hand around Jennifer's shoulder in a caretaking fashion while the other gingerly smoothed her old, navy blue skirt which had escaped the tyranny of an iron. Over her frumpy white blouse she'd draped her standard item of daily apparel—an old, gray sweater.

I struggled with my own longing to comfort my baby but

intuitively knew that there was something profoundly healing for her in the scene that was unfolding before me. Moving slowly toward the unlikely pair, I strained to hear what was being said.

"She'll never come back to life," Jennie's voice cracked. Then sobbing, added, "I'll never get to play with her again." Tears cascaded freely down her anguished little face. She gently and lovingly stroked the towel that hung in her arms, its motionless weight evidence of its lifeless content. Leaning closer, the old woman pulled the sleeve of her blouse into the palm of her hand and dabbed at Jennie's tears.

"It'll be okay," the old woman offered, trying to console the bereaved child. It was a feeble attempt at soothing the little girl and both she and Jennie knew it.

"You don't understand," my Jennie mumbled through her sobs, shaking her head from side to side. Now her feet were nonstop motion, swinging back and forth, back and forth, banging the underside of the park bench. Tears streaming and nose running, her grief welled up from a place deep inside and spilled over her memories of the joy of the rambunctious kitty in her arms, in her bed, at play. Agonized, she asked ever so sadly and slowly, "I loved Pumpkin and she loved me. *Why* did my kitty have to die?"

Experience told me that my Jennie wasn't really looking for an answer. Dabbing at my daughter's tears with the sleeve of her blouse, the old woman offered one anyway. "Maybe God needed your cat in heaven." As she spoke, her hand—covered with as many brown spots as it had porcelain colored skin—reached into her blouse and brought forth a

white handkerchief. Any self-consciousness long since forgotten, her movements were now the brisk, efficiently loving motions of a seasoned mother. She wiped Jennie's
running nose, then returned the handkerchief to where
she'd retrieved it.

"God doesn't need cats in heaven," Jennifer countered in
disgust. "Cats are given to us by God to play with and to
take care of." I thought it a rather interesting interpretation
of the value and reason for a cat's existence. I wondered
what the source of my daughter's information was and
what process she had used to formulate her philosophy.

"Oh, I know," the old woman said, trying to salvage her
reputation. She removed Jennie's baseball cap and stroked
the little girl's long sun-bleached auburn hair. Moments
passed before the old woman spoke again. A far-off look
came over her face and in a pining voice she whispered, "If
only she had been home where she belonged." I later
learned that mother and daughter had another of their
explosive arguments. The daughter had run from the house,
slamming the door behind her. She was just 17 at the time.

I watched, my feet refusing to interrupt this unusual
moment between this little girl who was grieving the loss
of her beloved cat and the old woman who was obviously
grieving the loss of her own beloved.

Perhaps feeling guilty, Jennie said, "If only I had taken care
of her this morning like I was supposed to, she wouldn't have
gone so far away. I was late for school so I didn't put food out
for her. Probably she got so hungry that she went hunting for
food. If only I had fed her this morning. If I . . . ." Remorsefully,
she shook her head from side to side.

Apparently, this was precisely what the old woman was thinking. *If only I had taken better care of the relationship between us; if only I had backed off when I knew my daughter was at her wit's end, if only . . . if only . . . then my daughter would still be alive. If only I had taken the time to understand, to talk, to explain. If only . . .*

"If only," Jennie continued and then stopped once again. Helplessness and hopelessness of the cat's death took over and she shouted in an angry voice, "My kitty is dead!"

At the same instant when my feet finally agreed to go to my little Jennifer to hold her and to comfort her, the old woman reached out and pulled my daughter to her bosom. Then the old woman bowed her head and began crying, too.

Startled, my daughter sat upright and asked, "Why are you crying?"

"Because she was so precious to me," the old woman said, now dabbing her own tears.

Jennifer was surprised by this response. After all, the old woman had on many occasions yelled at the cat and sometimes at my daughter when she saw the cat scouting in the neighborhood. Disbelieving what she heard and trying to bridge the duplicity between the old woman's past actions and, now, this caring remark, my daughter said, "But you were always yelling at her."

"Oh, I know," the old woman admitted. "If only I could do it over. If only I wouldn't have said those unkind things, perhaps she wouldn't have gone away, if only . . . If only I could take it back." With one hand she brushed away her own tears and with the other resumed stroking Jennie's hair.

"It wasn't *all* your fault," zodiac's healer said. Now, it was Jennie offering consolation.

"I guess it was the both of us," the old woman said resolutely, slowly nodding her head in agreement.

"Yup," Jennie said with a big sigh, perhaps deciding she would let the old woman own a bit of the guilt she felt over Pumpkin's poor treatment, perhaps even finding a bit of relief in sharing the burden of her belief that the cat might still be alive had she not neglected to feed it that morning. Moving to a stage of resolution, the tomboy pitcher with the best spitball in the city said, "Mom says blaming doesn't solve problems. It won't bring her back to life."

"Oh, I know," agreed the old-again woman nodding her head. "That's what my husband keeps saying. 'Forgive and forget,' that's what he says." She lifted her head, once again aware of the child, and said, "I'm sure your mother will get you another kitten."

"I don't want another kitten," Jennifer said defiantly. She swiftly rocked the dead kitten she cradled in her arms and resumed kicking the underside of the park bench. "No one can take her place!"

Remembering the conversation I'd overheard the night I rescued Pumpkin from the tree, I knew this was precisely what the old woman felt. No one could take the place of her dearly beloved daughter, not even the dutiful son.

"Yes," the old woman said sadly. *Nothing* could take her place. Tears from the place where she had locked them away came tumbling out of her weary old eyes. Choking them back, she squeaked, "We must not cry," as though by saying so she could will the tears back into the reservoir from whence they came. The tears came anyway, clouding her vision. Clumsy fingers pummeled the cloth on the tattered old sleeve searching for a dry spot, but no dry spot remained.

"When you're sad, crying is good for you," Jennifer counseled, patting the old woman's hand as she spoke. "Mom says it helps you shed sadness."

The old woman was surprised at the wisdom of a child so small. "Oh?" she said trying to sound confident. "Well, I've cried so much already. Maybe it's time for me to stop." Obviously she had been sad for so many years and was growing tired of her sadness.

Jennifer must have been impressed. "Really?" she asked.

"Oh, yes," said the old woman.

"I just want it to stop hurting," Jennifer said matter-of-factly.

"Yes, me too," agreed the old woman. "I long for it to stop hurting so much, too."

"Where does it hurt you?" questioned the little girl. "I hurt here the most." Jennifer placed her hand on her stomach.

"My ache lives here in my chest," responded the old woman. "And deep within my heart." The old woman placed an angry fist on her bosom but as she moved the clenched hand to her heart region, it opened. It was an open palm with a light and loving touch that greeted her heart. She paused, and then added thoughtfully, "Sometimes I just hurt all over." Her hand made a broad overall swooshing motion from her head to her feet.

"They didn't stop to see if they had hurt her," my daughter said softly.

"Ooooh, it was so awful," the old woman shuddered. Once again overcome by her misery, the old woman retracted the arm from around Jen's shoulder. She put both arms around herself and rocked back and forth. Her daughter's body had been found nearly six hours after the hit-and-run, an insult she could never bridge.

"It was hours later," the old woman cried softly, still rocking back and forth.

"And no one came to her rescue," my daughter said factually, no longer refusing to accept the events and circumstances surrounding her kitten's death.

"Oh, I know," the old woman murmured. "If only I could have been there for her."

"I don't think it would have mattered," offered Jennifer. "Nothing could have survived being hit by a fast car."

"I can't bear to think about that," the old woman railed, the vision of her daughter's body coming into sharp focus as clear as the day it happened. "You must forgive and forget," she said. But the vision was too powerful and refused to be set aside. The message meant for the little girl beside her knocked wildly at the door to her own battered heart and called out to her, "You, too, must forgive." It seemed time to lean into this feeling rather than move from it. With one hand flattened against her forehead and the other hand used to hold her face, the old woman hung her head, and wept and wept.

Instinctively, Jennifer reached out and put her little arms around the round, tiny gray-haired woman. Instinctively, the old woman responded in kind, wrapping her own arms around the child. The old woman's head rested on top of Jen's,

Jen's head rested against the old woman's chest. They clung to each other, gently swaying back and forth, and simply held each other in silence for what seemed like a very long time.

As the power of compassion that danced between them—lingering where it was most needed at the moment—offered succor and depleted their grief, the two stirred slowly. Patting Jennie's head, the old woman sat up and asked, "Do you want me to help you bury your kitty?"

"Yup," said Jennie enthusiastically. "I want to bury her here beneath this tree." She pointed to the same tree from which I rescued Pumpkin, full of lush leaves, green and vibrant from the spring rains. Looking tenderly into the old woman's eyes Jennie asked earnestly, "My Sunday School teacher says that when you die, only the soul goes on to heaven. Exactly what part of my kitty will go to heaven?"

Covering all the bases, the old woman offered up cheerfully, "The way you loved your kitty, and the way she loved you, I wouldn't be a bit surprised if *all* of her went to heaven."

I watched as the two of them dug the hole, alternating between an adult's knowing and a child's sense of the size of hole required. "Isn't this much bigger than what's needed?" Jennie asked kneeling. The old woman smiled, but said nothing. She dug deeper. Jennie understood the old woman's quiet sweetness. She watched in silence.

Finally, the old woman looked up at Jen and nodded. Jennie carefully unfolded the towel and gazed at her kitten for the last time. She gently stroked Pumpkin's long silky fur, her teary eyes drinking in this final sight of her beloved playmate. She then lay her little head on Pumpkin's broken body and kissed it delicately before carefully wrapping it again in the towel. As Jennie kneeled to lay her kitten to rest, the old woman stopped her. "Wait . . . wait just a minute," she said slowly. With painstaking precision, she quickly removed her trademark sweater and placed it in Jennifer's hand. "Use this in place of the towel," she instructed.

"But why?" asked Jennie. "Mom won't mind that this towel isn't returned."

"It's more than that," the old woman said. Her eyes reddened from sobbing, she explained, "This is the sweater I was wearing when they found her body. Maybe I shouldn't wear it anymore." Her lips trembled as she sniffed and wiped away tears. Then she went on, "It painfully reminds me of her. I want to do what you're doing, to have sweet memories of love, not bitter memories of pain." She looked away from Jen, who watched and listened attentively. The old woman looked back, nodded and said, "It's time I forgive, like you did today." Heaving a heavy sigh, she added, "It's time to bury my grief."

Reverently, as in a sacred ceremony, the two exchanged the towel for the sweater—each for different reasons. Both Jennie and the old woman kneeled and stroked the sweater one last time, willingly offering up their precious goods—each for the same reason. Each entrusted to Mother Earth their special, though separate, memories.

The incident transformed the old woman. For the next few weeks, she often knocked at my door to ask if Jennifer could go for a walk with her. From time to time, the old woman and I talked briefly about that day. In accordance to what she was ready to disclose, she shared the story of her loss and grief. These visits were brief; it was Jennifer she needed, not me. Jennifer seemed to need time with the old woman almost as much as the old woman needed her.

Although the old man and Jen never had the same bond his wife shared with my daughter, he welcomed Jennie into their home and their life. He was overjoyed with the change in his wife and knew her relationship with Jennie had something to do with it.

The incident definitely changed the relationship between the old man and his wife. There wasn't the same amount of bickering and moaning and groaning between them after that afternoon. They actually walked companionably across the condominium's well-landscaped grounds from time to time, not a word of criticism or complaint between them. No longer bound by their need to focus on each other's faults in order to deal with their individual pain, they now took separate walks as well. The old woman always preferred to take these walks with Jennie.

Walking and talking time turned into helping with homework time, and the old woman became more and more protective of Jennifer. She preferred taking her walk in the vicinity of my daughter's school around the time that my daughter was leaving to walk the six blocks home. This went on for the next two years, until I bought a house and moved from the condominium complex.

The old woman is now a really old woman. Still, my daughter calls on her and is protective of her. Jennie now wants to know the qualifications of those in charge of her care now that she is widowed and living in a seniors' home.

Having reached out and shared in each other's grief, Jennie and the old woman formed a lasting bond. Perhaps it was this reaching outside of herself to comfort a grieving child—with no other motive than to help someone else in pain—that finally allowed the old woman to begin healing. One thing is certain, she is a very loving woman now, and, in being so, she has no room left for bitterness.

2

Third-Place Winner

*The best educated human being is
the one who understands most about the
life in which he is placed.*

—Helen Keller

His head lowered, an exhausted but determined young
man chanted over and over to himself, "*You* can do this.
You *can* do it, *you* can do it, you *can do it.*" These words,
spoken as much for encouragement as for confirmation,
found a listening heart. Without fail they drove one foot in
front of the other, up into the air and then down—again

and again and again. The boy watched intently as one by one, each of his new sneakers methodically slapped the asphalt slowly passing beneath him. It was a *very* tired patter. Looking up, the youth wiped his brow and searched for a glimpse of the finish line. "It's somewhere up there," he told himself matter-of-factly.

It was far off in the distance. Even so, Chris Burke had his heart set on reaching it.

With great effort, he, too, crossed the finish line. By the time he did, photographers and reporters had already gathered around the young man who had taken first place. Cameras zoomed in and flashed; microphones stretched forward to absorb the winner's words.

With a smile that stretched from ear to ear, Chris jubilantly bounded over and proudly stood next to the winner. He wrapped his arm around the young man his own age— someone he had never met prior to this event. Beaming, Chris patiently waited for the reporter to complete his interview with the victor—as patiently as he could in a moment that held so much excitement for him. When at last the reporter turned to the camera to make concluding remarks, Chris instantly stepped forward and thrust out his hand to receive a congratulatory handshake. "Oh, boy!" Chris shouted, unable to restrain his obvious joy. "I just want to tell you what a thrill this was and how happy I am to have come in third!" The reporter had little choice but to respond to the charismatic and enthusiastic athlete, wanting *his* turn at recognition.

"Yes . . . tell us about it," stammered the startled reporter good-naturedly.

"Wow!" said Chris. "Thank you for asking me to be interviewed. This is great! Just great. Well, I'm just very happy to be here. It's such a great honor. Of course, I finished in third place. Third place, not bad! Not bad, huh?" He didn't need an answer to his question, and he didn't wait for one. Instead, he turned his animated face for all of the world to see—this *was* national television—and with more joy than I can remember from anyone, he said, "Thank you all for sharing in this very special time with me. It's time to celebrate!" With that, Chris turned, and ran over to line up for hugs and handshakes alongside the winner.

Chris was 14 years old at the time. This was the Special Olympics.

There were only three runners in the entire race!

To appreciate the full significance of Chris' story, one must recognize Chris has Down's syndrome, a condition caused by a gene malfunction. Down's children are born with one too many chromosomes, resulting in an uncanny similarity in appearance, thwarted development and a ceiling on potential. Since IQ peaks out at around 75, capability and ability are severely limited—or so it was thought. When Chris was born in 1965, physicians recommended that parents place Down's babies in institutions, the majority of which did little more than offer physical caretaking.

Most of the world now knows Chris Burke not only from his unforgettable interview years ago, but also as the charismatic and gifted television actor and star of the television series, *Life Goes On*. The show enjoyed four years of excellent ratings. This very special young man has surged well beyond the commonly held assumptions of those with Down's syndrome. He has, in fact, created a new reality for himself.

I wanted to know this young man.

You need only meet Chris Burke for a moment to feel the power of his presence and share in the glee of his unmistakable wit. "How does it feel to have Down's syndrome?" I asked him.

"I don't think of it as Down's syndrome," he replied blissfully. "I call it *Up* syndrome!"

"How so?" I inquired, hoping he would shed more light on his extraordinary and genuinely sunny outlook on life.

Without a moment's hesitation he confidently replied, "Up has provided some real opportunities that I might not have had." He looked pensive for a moment and added, "It's been a gift, really."

"A gift?" I questioned.

He replied instantly, "The talents that you have are God's gift to you." He looked at me with clear steely-blue eyes—eyes that held no hidden agenda, eyes incapable of *not* smiling. "What you do with them is your gift to God."

"Robert Schuller, right?" I asked.

"Exactly!" he said laughing. He pointed to a small slab of granite encased in a lovely frame of pewter sitting on his desk with Schuller's words engraved on it.

"What obstacles have you had to overcome?" I asked, pressing on. He looked almost surprised at my question, then pointed to a framed poster on his wall with the words, "Obstacles are what you see when you take your eyes off the goal." He grinned and said, "I try never to take my eyes off my goal!"

"Which is aspiring to be a full-time actor?" I asked.

After a deep rich laugh, he said sheepishly, "Oh, I'm already an actor, and a good one." Then, with more sincerity than amusement, he remarked, "My goal is to live life to the fullest and, in the meantime, develop my potential." He grinned broadly and added, "That may take awhile! Right now, I'm pretty excited about what I'm doing, which is, editor in chief of the National Down's Syndrome Society magazine."

True to form, Chris tirelessly devotes energy to a daily schedule in making his new dream—creating a magazine to expand awareness and understanding of Down's syndrome—come true. This very special and much-needed national magazine is very successful. Seeing how jazzed up he became by the mere mention of this new project, I asked Chris, "What do you think is the secret behind the magazine's success?"

"We're successful because we talk about what works," he explained. "We don't dwell on the negatives. Ever notice how the front page of the newspaper highlights man's downfalls while the sports page highlights his victories? We're going to highlight victories! It's much more useful to know what works than what doesn't."

"And what about for you, Chris?" I asked. "What made the difference? How is it that *you* have achieved so much?"

"I'm not so very different from others," he said without hesitation. "My parents didn't treat me any differently than my brothers and sisters. They insisted that I be self-reliant. Achievement was expected. They wanted me to stand on my own two feet. And that's what I wanted, too."

"You possess so much joy," I remarked, but before I could finish the question I had intended to ask him, he answered it by saying, "That's what makes it so easy to do things."

"Do you think we underestimate the importance of joy?" I asked.

"Absolutely, no question. And the power of it," responded this delightful young man. "If you have joy, you'll work hard to see your dream come true."

I'm always amazed at the size, color and vividness of the picture Chris holds of himself. I also know how important this image is in dwarfing the obstacles he encounters—and overcomes—in achieving his goals. I think about the teachings of great scholars—from Plato, Socrates and Aristotle, to Maria Montessori and Jaime Escalante—and the legacy they left: the keys to discovery and a thirst for lifelong questing and learning. I'm certain that what Chris knows is a piece of the puzzle—and should shake up our notion of potential. It reminds us of our responsibility to support all humans as they go about their itinerary, no matter how different the route in getting there.

Captivated by his charisma and joy, I asked, "What makes you *most* happy?"

"My dad always says that happiness is the result of doing the things we find most value in doing," he replied.

"My father made a similar statement," I said. "His version went something like this, 'Find something you love to do, align your goals and be willing to spend the time it takes to accomplish it.'"

"Yup," said Chris, "when you're doing what you like to do, it puts a smile on your face." He grinned that unmistakable Burke smile and added, "I want to produce and direct a movie next. It's just a matter of time." Suddenly his eyes lit up and he said, "Hey, send me the story you're doing on me. I could play me—what a great idea. Boy, that would be fun. Steven Spielberg could direct it. I plan to have dinner with him when I'm in California. Seriously, he's the very best director there is. He's my mentor. I want to be as good a director as he is." Laughing like a grizzly bear gargling through honey, Chris added, "Someday, I will."

"Are there no limits, Chris?"

"What?" he asked, truly not understanding how to answer my question. It's obvious that his mind was at work "directing." "You know," he gushed, "my parents could play themselves in the movie!"

"I can tell you really admire your parents," I said.

"Sure do. They're great. How about you? Do you admire your parents?"

"Without a doubt, Chris," I said, now finding myself in the role of interviewee. "I love and greatly admire them."

"Did they teach you to 'go for it'?"

"Yes, they did," I said smiling, feeling joyous just by being in this young man's presence. "Dad always used the line, 'Passion is the reflection of your work radiating your heart's desires.'"

"When you like your work," Chris said with certainty, "it's more fun than work. Like when I wrote my book, *A*

Special Kind of Hero. I wanted to do it, so even though it was a big job, I got it done. I did it."

"I couldn't agree more, Chris."

"I think life is to have fun. And to *do* something fun," Chris volunteered. He looked at me earnestly and asked, "Are *you* having fun? You look like you are."

"I sure am, Chris," I replied.

Continuing his light-hearted interrogation, he asked, "Do you enjoy what you do?"

"Yes, again. I love every minute of it!"

"Well, then," said Chris, "maybe you'll be able to accomplish something worthwhile, too!"

I thought about Chris and my conversation with him for some time. His joy is contagious, his enthusiasm real. Both are a key to his achievement and satisfaction. Chris was guided early in life to think without self-imposed limitations and to continually upgrade the expectations he holds for himself. As a result, Chris is busy discovering his potential. He deeply believes this will take some time to find. Fun is the route; joy and satisfaction the outcome. Using his gifts, Chris is going beyond what many others thought possible of him. Interestingly, it's not outside the scope of what he expects of himself.

Chris may have been a third-place winner many years ago, but today his life holds the "best prize." Chris has found a place where his specialness can shine, where differences can be expressed and where a mind can support a heart working freely and fully.

Author's note: When talking with Chris after this interview, he mentioned that he had been included in Robert Pamtlin's book, *American Heroes*. "I'm listed first," he said to me. "They put the story about me first!"

"Wow, Chris," I said, impressed. "That's great."

"That's because the stories appear in alphabetical order," interjected his mother, smiling. Wryly she added, "And your name starts with B, Chris. It's a coincidence."

Chris looked at his mother lovingly and gently pointed to the words in a mahogany frame above his desk: "Everything—and everyone—has a reason for being."

3 Houndoggie

*Love is the irresistible desire
to be irresistibly desired.*

—Robert Frost

With one hand flat against the thick pane of glass and the other on her knee, an elderly woman in an ample, rose-colored knee-length coat stooped down to get closer to the puppy caged within the storefront's display window. Her face was pressed so close to the glass that little clouds of mist appeared and disappeared on its surface with each breath she expended. In a sweet, playful child's voice she quizzed, "What's your name? I'll bet it's Houndoggie, isn't it? I'll bet it is. Is that it, huh?" Enchanted by her affectionate attention, the baby dachshund trapped behind the glass could hardly restrain himself. A whirlwind of excited motion, he wagged his tail frantically, yipped, moaned and furiously licked the window, desperate to get closer to the woman and her affection. Standing on his hind legs, the exuberant pup thrust his elongated yet rounded little belly taut against the pane and stretched his stubby, muscular front legs as high up as he could get on the glass.

"*Yeees*, you'd like to come out to play *wouldn't* you?" she cooed in a grandmotherly fashion. "Yeees. You're a little lover, aren't you?" Frenzied by his frustrated glee, the little puppy's thick flesh-padded front paws alternately thumped, scratched and slid against the slick surface of the glass. "Oh, yeeees," she acknowledged again, and then informed him, "I once had a doggie that looked *just like you*. My Herbert, bless his soul, named our puppy Horace, but I called that doggie, *Houndoggie*. What a wonderful companion he was."

Listening intently to the melodic tone of her voice, the baby dachshund cocked his head to the side and looked her in the eyes. He knew he had found the pot of gold at the end of the rainbow; he need only get to it. Agitated by his pent-up affection, the puppy trampolined up and down yet again. Finally, so topsy-turvy was his joy, the little dog twirled around and around in frustrated delight.

"I sure wish *you* were *my* puppy," she said to him. "Oh, how I'd love you. And you'd love me right back, wouldn't you? My Herbert always said, 'What goes around comes around.'" Momentarily tired out by his fervent performance of merriment, the little puppy leaned firmly but quietly against the glass, a total picture of yearning. The woman savored the moment, too. In her face I saw a mother's unending love. Her heart smitten, the elderly woman removed her hand from her knee and with it traced the outline of his healthy little body. As though the little guy knew that being united with his new love was hopeless, a look of defeat swept over his large brown eyes. Unable to lick the warm hands denied him by the window pane, his tongue settled for long slow passionate swipes of cold tasteless glass.

With a loving look of longing on her face, the woman hurried into the pet store.

Witnessing their tryst, I believed that the puppy had found a new mother that day. The memory of Houndoggie would now have a rival. With a feeling of lighthearted satisfaction I continued on my way.

Two weeks later when I went back to purchase supplies for my pets, there was a different sort of commotion going on at the display window. This time all the activity came from outside the storefront where two store employees were busy trying to create a work of art for Cupid's holiday. Peering past them, I noticed that "Houndoggie" was gone. Sold, I presumed, to the woman I had seen admiring him. Two obviously frightened fawn-colored bunnies with suspicious eyes now huddled in the corner, their watchful stare darting to and fro. They looked first at the two humans painting hearts, Cupids and other symbols of love on the glass window, then at the flickers of passersby.

Nearly everyone stopped to view the display. Parents found themselves yanked to the window by the persistent tug of children. These same parents sealed their fate if their response to the obvious follow-up query from their little ones was, "Yes, we can go inside to look, but just for a minute." Having gone in just for a closer look, many of these mere window shoppers came out carrying bundles of new-found love in their arms or in newly purchased carrying cages, their lives changed forever. This was especially true for the children, most of whom had little foresight as to how a pet would give new meaning to the word *responsibility* and would alter the once peaceful relations between them and their parents.

Looking at the bunnies, I thought, poor little sweethearts. In concert with the rapid rhythm of their stressful breathing, the little bunnies' tiny nostrils flared in and out, in and out, keeping perfect harmony with the quick, steady rise and fall of their panting bodies.

As I was leaving this pet shop one week later, I saw the old woman again. Just as she had when I had first noticed her weeks ago, she was wearing a bulky rose-colored coat and peering into the store's display window. She was again cajoling the "please-take-me-home-with-you" object of the week in the window. "What's your name, Houndoggie? Wouldn't you like somebody to love? If you were my dog, I'd make you such a fine home," she teased.

I was puzzled. I hadn't noticed anything in the display window on my way into the store. Several days prior, the bunnies had been replaced by a litter of five kittens that had successfully entertained passersby. In only two days all five kittens had enchanted themselves into the lives of new owners. Since the display window was so large, it was easy to see what was inside. I was sure this space was empty today, but hearing the older woman's conversation, I assumed a dog had been placed in the display case while I was in the store. Since I was curious, I walked over to get a look at what breed of dog was on display. I could see *no* living thing in the space inside the window. Perhaps there was a gerbil, a snake or a miniature dog in the window. Perhaps *this* Houndoggie was hiding under the mounds of red shredded paper. Perhaps he'd jumped into the container that held heart-shaped balloons and decorative gifts in the window's corner.

I examined every possible square inch of the window display. There was simply *no* dog there. The old woman was just pretending. Turning to her, I said softly so as not to startle her, "Hi. So, what do they have in there this week?"

"Oh, hello," she said, turning to me and returning my greeting. She seemed undisturbed that I had overheard her talking to her phantom puppy, but she did not address my question.

I tried once again. "I thought I heard you talking to a dog. I don't see a doggie in there, do *you?*" I was really interested in what she would say. I wondered if, for her, the dog really did exist or if momentarily she merely hoped it did.

"No one could ever take care of Houndoggie as I would," she replied in a rather somber tone, still ignoring my question. Though she'd sounded cheerful just seconds before, now her voice resonated sadness. Her next statement showed me that she really did know the difference between fantasy and reality. "It was love at first sight," she said in a schoolgirl's voice. "Oh, I *really* wanted him. A dog is such a good companion when you're alone. It's been three years since my dear husband Herbert died and it'll be a year this Valentine's Day since my Houndoggie died." She paused and then said tenderly, "I miss them so much. I would love to get another dog . . ." Her sweet disposition couldn't hide her first-degree sadness.

Remembering the passionate exchange I had seen between her and the dog some weeks back, and assuming she meant *that* "Houndoggie" and not the imaginary one that was here today, I inquired, "Why didn't you buy the dachshund that was here a few weeks ago? If you really want a dog, you should have one."

"Oh," she lamented, "he was so *very* expensive." She became momentarily quiet before adding, "I'm afraid my pension just won't stretch that far." Suddenly a look of delight crossed her face and she said enthusiastically, "Puppies, so rambunctious! They can be a handful, can't they?" These words made her eyes sparkle. She paused again and then added thoughtfully, "Probably I should have a grown dog and not a puppy, anyway. It would be easier for me to care for."

As quickly as this optimism appeared, it disappeared. She pulled her coat tightly around her, folded her arms high across her chest, sighed deeply and said resolutely, "But, it looks like I won't be getting either." Her eyes moist, she turned to scuttle away. Not forgetting her manners, she called over her shoulder, "You have a nice day."

With Valentine's Day now just days away, festive signs proclaiming news of "sweetheart" sales were posted on the display case and hung throughout the store. Newly adorned with red streamers, hearts and papier-mâché Cupids, the display window showcased two wrinkle-faced Shar-pei puppies at play. I paused to admire them, then went into the store to purchase dog food for Domino, my 10-year-old dalmatian.

Having thought often of the sweet little lady and her yearning for a dog since the last time I'd been in, I spoke to the store owner as I paid for my purchases. "Several weeks ago I saw an older lady admiring a dachshund in the storefront window," I said. "She seems to want a pet very badly. Have you noticed her?"

"Oh, yeah," the manager said. "She's just an old nutty woman. She hangs around here. A nuisance really."

"How so?" I inquired, surprised that someone in his position—who needed to be intuitive with humans and sensitive to animals—would make such a comment.

"Oh," he said in an exasperated tone, "apparently she wants a dachshund because every time there's one in the window or in the shop, she comes in nearly every day to pet and fondle it. But she's not a serious buyer, so I try to chase her away so she doesn't annoy the customers. If she bothered you in any way, I'm very sorry."

"She wasn't a bother," I said matter-of-factly. I was disturbed by the duplicity of his being in the business of bringing human and animal together, yet showing such little empathy for this woman's plight. "I was just wondering how we might help her."

"*Help* her?" he chuckled, making fun of her peculiar ways. "A pet isn't the only kind of help she needs!" Finding his humor at her expense more disrespectful than funny I said, "I don't find her *odd*, just longing to have a pet in her life." Wondering if I might convince him to allow her to buy a dog at a reduced rate, I asked politely, "I noticed your Valentine's Day sale signs; what kind of a discount are you offering on your dachshunds?"

"The sale doesn't apply to animals, just merchandise," he answered. "I only lower the price on animals if they aren't selling quickly."

"Oh," I said, wanting to know more. "Does it ever happen that a dachshund doesn't sell right away?"

"Oh, sure, every now and then," he replied, "especially if we get one in that isn't desirable. Last week I had to turn in two such animals."

"Turn in?" I questioned. "What happens when an animal is *turned in?*"

"We might give it to the Humane Society," he said.

"Oh," I remarked. Still curious, I asked, "Do *you* make those decisions?"

"I make all the decisions around here!" he said smartly.

"So," I said, deciding to use his highly rated sense of power as leverage, "*you* make a decision as to whether or not you want to sell an animal or donate it to some sort of charity?"

"Uh-huh," he said, as yet unaware of where I was leading him.

"I see," I said, edging closer to piecing together a plan that might help secure a dog for the woman. "So this isn't a franchise then, it's your very own store, right?"

"I'm the man!" he said, playing right into my hand.

Going for the close, I zeroed in, "That means *you* could make a decision to give one to the older woman, if you like?"

"Well," he said gruffly, finally realizing what I was on to, "I can't just let the public know that if an animal stays in my store long enough, I'll give it away. That would be bad for business, now wouldn't it? I'd have a waiting list of people standing in line for a free animal. I can't make a living that way."

I could see that if I wanted to get him to soften his position and participate in resolving the dogless woman's dilemma, I would need to change my tone. I thought for a moment of the most persuasive technique I had witnessed: immediately my daughter's style came to mind. Yes, of course, I should switch to the approach my daughter always used with me—it was time-honored and worked every time. I'd start with the butter-up, then go for guilt and finish with pleadings that went straight to the heart.

Hoping my intended look of innocence was projected and as convincing as when my daughter used it on me, I said, "Mr. Meaghers, you have the best selection of the nicest animals anywhere in this city." Moving from victim to professional, he smiled and said, "Why thank you, Dr. Youngs."

"I know it must give you great satisfaction when an animal and a new owner are leaving your store *together*, both happy and thrilled with each other," I gushed. Remembering the Member of the Chamber of Commerce emblem in his window on the way in, I added, "I see you're a member of the Chamber. I am too." With both hands on his hips, Mr. Meaghers stood at attention listening to my every word. I hurried on. "Their February theme of 'Have a Heart: Show Your Community You Care—Assist Someone in Need,' is a worthy goal, isn't it?"

"I'll say," he agreed.

"Come to think of it," I added, "that elderly lady who keeps coming in here because she *longs* to have a dog, the one living on a limited income, well, helping someone like her would certainly achieve the sentiment of their motto, wouldn't it? She's so alone and pining to replace her dog. She hasn't had any luck finding one advertised 'to a good home' in the newspaper. Just think what a great pet owner that lady would be and how fortunate for the puppy to have her as a doting mother. Since her dog died nearly a year ago—on Valentine's Day no less—this time of the year must be even more lonely for her. Oh, Mr. Meaghers, there must be a way *you* can be instrumental in helping this poor lady." Playfully, yet sincerely, I added, "With it being the season for giving and all, it sure would be a Valentine kind of thing to do."

Not waiting for me to continue, Mr. Meaghers interjected, "It's her family's obligation to help her out, not mine."

"I gather she may not have family here," I countered. "She lost her husband some years back."

Mr. Meaghers remained unmoved. He said, "I don't have the power to do what you're asking."

I could tell it was useless. Upon leaving the store I mumbled, *"You never know how much power you have until you use it,* that's what my father always said."

I re-ran this conversation between the pet store owner and myself over and over in my mind for the next two days.

One morning, it dawned on me that my thinking was fraught with error: why should it be the pet store owner's duty to fulfill the elderly woman's desire to have a dog? Why was I abdicating my role in being a good Samaritan? Why had I assigned it to be *his* responsibility to play Cupid? Why spend time and energy trying to persuade him of the joy of giving, when I should be doing this? Why not me?

I called the store manager and asked if he knew how to get in touch with the elderly woman. "No, but with my luck, she'll no doubt be in before the end of the week," he said in mockery.

"When will you get more dachshunds in?" I asked.

"Tuesday, the 12th," came the reply.

"What are you asking for them?"

"Three hundred and twenty-five dollars each," was the answer.

No wonder the elderly lady couldn't afford one, I thought. "I'd like you to take down my credit card number," I said. "And call that lady and let her have the pick of the litter."

"Really?" he asked. "You shouldn't have to do this."

"There doesn't seem to be anyone else who can change her fate, Mr. Meaghers," I replied. "There is no Valentine in her life. A puppy will be a nice start. Besides, it seems like a very small good deed to do for someone needing and wanting a puppy to love—though I do remember her saying that an adult dog would be easier for her to care for. Anyway, I'm sorry for trying to make you feel as though it was your responsibility. I'm the one filled with feelings of her loss; it's my responsibility to help her replace her dog.

It's a small thing in the scheme of things, though believe me I have other things I would like to do with $325. But this seems like a necessary purchase. I'll come by tomorrow and sign the credit card slip."

On the way into his store the next day, I noticed over to the side in the decorated display window, a beautiful, two-year-old, chestnut brown dachshund. Her dark eyes sparkled as she bounded up to the glass. She wore a big red bow to one side of her neck. Her tail wagged merrily as she inspected me while I inspected her. Though not nearly as rambunctious as her younger predecessor had been, she had a warm and friendly disposition. I thought she'd be just perfect for the elderly woman. Looking over to the corner of the display area, I saw a pile of pooch paraphernalia: a wicker dog bed lined in red flannel; at least a month's supply of dog food; an elaborate wooden doghouse, painted white with windows trimmed with large and small red hearts, with a gigantic red velvet bow tied across it; and tumbling from the door of the festive doghouse was an assortment of pet toys. The sign in the window said "sold."

Once inside the store, a cheerful and very excited Mr. Meaghers greeted me. "Did you see her? Did you see her? She's beautiful, a real sweetheart isn't she?" he chirped.

"The dachshund in the display case?" I asked, going for clarification. The dog in the display window was an adult dog, not a puppy. Uh-oh, I thought, wondering if I was just about to sign on the dotted line for *all* the things I had seen in the storefront window, wondering exactly how much had been charged on my card.

"Yes," he said excitedly. "I remembered you mentioning that our friend would rather have a grown dog, so I made some calls. I ran across a really special situation where someone was wanting to sell a two-year-old dachshund. I looked her over and, seeing how nice she was, decided she was perfect for our lady friend." I took note that all of a sudden she was "our" friend. He went on, "A dog like this goes for nearly $250 with full papers, which this one has."

"She's really beautiful," I said, admiring the friendly and very healthy-looking dog. It occurred to me that he had just confirmed that I had purchased not only the $250 dog, but all these items. "Well," I said laughing nervously, "I'm very happy you found this dog and I do think the dog food is a necessity, but I think she can devise her own toys and makeshift bed. Probably she'll keep her indoors and won't be needing the very large doghouse."

"Not to worry," he said, handing me a torn-in-half credit card slip. "It's on me. I thought about it and it's only right to help her out. Besides," he said smiling broadly, "you never know how much power you have until you use it."

Four months later I was surprised to see two dachshund puppies frolicking in the display window with a posted "Free to a good home" sign. Perhaps the store manager changed his policy, I thought, or perhaps the store is under new management. I remembered how earlier he said it wasn't good to set such a precedent.

I went inside and inquired.

"No one knew the dachshund our lady friend received was with pups," Mr. Meaghers said with a grin. "Why, two months after being taken home, that dachshund promptly delivered three puppies. Come, look." He happily opened the wire cage to let me hold them. Tails wagging, their warm little bodies squirmed with delight as one by one they basked in my attention. Each one affectionate, they oozed love, health and the scent of puppy breath.

The elderly woman had taken them to the pet store. She allowed Mr. Meaghers the pick of the litter with the instructions that it was his to sell, but the other two were to be given away free.

"Said it was her 'giving back' for having received her 'Valentine'—that's what she named her dog," Mr. Meaghers said. Shrugging his shoulders he added, "She said, *What goes around, comes around.*'"

"What a wonderful outcome, Mr. Meaghers," I exclaimed. "And you made all this happen."

"Well," he said smiling ear-to-ear, "what goes around, comes around."

4

Ground Fog or Head Fog?

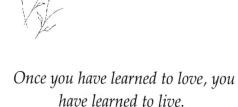

*Once you have learned to love, you
have learned to live.*

—Source Unknown

I looked at the exasperated traveler with the bulky brief-case and an even bigger sense of self-importance. "Going to Medford?" I asked.

"Damn right I'm going to Medford!" he declared.

"So, do you want to come along?" I invited.

"Hell no!" he stammered. "I'm not going to be cooped up with strangers and drive all night. This airline has

inconvenienced me, and they're going to make it right."
Slapping his airline tickets against his alligator-skin briefcase, he threatened, "Either that or they're going to refund
me the full price of a first-class ticket and I'll find another
airline who can keep their schedule!"

"Sir," asserted the pretty young agent behind the desk,
"I'm afraid we can't refund your ticket. The weather is not
our fault. The airline is not responsible for poor weather
conditions and is not liable in such circumstances."

This was more than the man could handle. His face reddened, veins bulged on his forehead and protruded from
his neck. "Where is the head supervisor?" he yelled. "It's
obvious you have no clout around here!"

I was traveling to keynote a national conference being
held at the convention center in Ashland, Oregon. I wanted
to spend as much time as possible with my daughter and
my busy office staff, so I had my travel agent book me on
the last flight from San Diego into the Portland, Oregon airport. From there I was to connect to a flight to Medford,
Oregon. I'd spend the evening there, then my conference
host would pick me up bright and early the next day and
drive me the remaining 10 or so miles into the beautiful
little village of Ashland, home of the renowned Oregon
Shakespeare Theater.

As scheduled, the plane departed the San Diego airport
at 7:30 P.M. for Portland. When our flight arrived in the
Portland area, the pilot informed us that due to dense
ground fog our plane had to join other aircraft circling the
Portland airport awaiting clearance to land. Luckily, our

plane landed and wasn't sent back to its originating destination (as were some carriers). Unfortunately, by the time we landed, the flight was nearly an hour late. I was concerned because late arrival meant I probably missed my connecting flight.

I hurried to the nearby monitor to confirm my fate, but was pleasantly surprised—and greatly relieved—to find that my connecting flight was delayed and had not yet departed. I quickly made my way to the check-in counter and took my place in line with other travelers securing boarding passes for this flight. Within moments the agent at the podium announced: "For passengers connecting with flight number 1418 to Medford, we have just learned that due to dense ground fog, this flight has been *canceled.* This is the only carrier that flies this route at this time of evening. We're sorry for any inconvenience this has caused you, and will do our best to assist you with securing a seat on the first flight out tomorrow morning. If you'll be patient, I'll do my best to help you make other reservations."

The faces of the passengers waiting in line for the canceled flight changed from somber to concerned. I stood still for a moment, sharing their dismay. While I pondered my dilemma, the well-dressed middle-aged man—unwilling to submit to forces beyond his far-reaching control—shoved his way to the front of the line of distraught travelers, slammed his briefcase on the counter and shouted, "How can you possibly cancel the flight? I've got to get to Medford *tonight!*"

"I'm very sorry, sir," said the agent behind the counter. She was a young woman of perhaps 24 or 25. Her dark blue uniform, along with her graceful confidence, granted her an aura of benevolent authority. The highlights in her neatly styled, shoulder-length blonde hair gleamed as, nodding sympathetically, she continued, "As I've just informed everyone, there are no other flights out tonight. The best we can do is to get you on the first flight out tomorrow."

"Tomorrow!" the man stammered with the same level of frustration the rest of us felt. "I can't wait until tomorrow! I have to get there tonight."

Her brown eyes conveyed genuine patience and compassion as she tried to console him. "I'm sorry, sir. This is a matter of fog, and no plane can take off in these conditions. The first flight out is at 6:55 A.M., getting into Medford at 8:00. There are still open seats. If you'll wait your turn in line, I can try to get you on that flight."

"I'm supposed to *be there* at 8:00," the man hollered. "I don't know about you, but I'm not accustomed to being late. There must be some sort of air transportation—private carriers perhaps. You need to find me an alternative and be quick about it!"

The young girl remained polite but enunciated clearly, "Sir, it's about the weather and there are no more flights this evening. They've all been canceled, so . . ."

"I've heard your damn excuses," he stormed. "I didn't ask you to give me a dissertation on why the plane is grounded. I asked you to get me to my destination *tonight*."

A *car*, I thought. I would have to get there by car. Interrupting the enraged man's tantrum, I called from my place in line, "Excuse me, ma'am. How many land miles to Medford?"

"It's about 260," the efficient agent replied. "About four and a half to five hours of driving time this hour of night."

I turned and looked into the line of stranded passengers. "I'm going to Medford by rental car, if I can get one," I announced. "Anyone want to . . ." Before I could finish, two men stepped forward.

"I live in Medford and I'd love to get home tonight," said the man closest to me, whose name was Bill. "But I'm afraid I'm not much of a night driver."

"I'll drive," volunteered the second man. "I need to get to Medford for business bright and early tomorrow, so I'd prefer to spend the night there rather than here. Nighttime driving doesn't bother me at all. By the way, my name is Jerry."

"If you drive," said Bill, "I'll pay your share of the rental car."

"That sounds just fine with me," said Jerry.

"It's a deal," I said. "Let's go get a car!"

That's when I asked the man at the counter if he wanted to come along. He told me in no uncertain terms that he had no intention of being cooped up with strangers during a drive to Medford. Then he turned his back to me and continued his tirade. "If you can't help me," he spat at the young woman, "then find someone who can. Where's your supervisor?"

Exchanging a polite demeanor for a more assertive one, the agent said, "Sir, I *am* the supervisor, the *only* one, and this is the only airline that flies from Portland to Medford."

"Well, then get me the head pilot," he badgered. "I need to talk to somebody who can do something about this mess."

"I'm right here," said a pilot, stepping into view, "and I'm afraid I'm in the same boat as you. This fog has caused quite a few dilemmas for me, too. Not getting to my next destination tonight means that my whole day tomorrow is askew."

"Well," huffed the man, "someone can take your place, but no one can take my place!"

"Yes, I suppose so," chuckled the pilot. "They will call in a replacement crew for me. But I'm sure your party will understand your predicament and make allowances. Sometimes we just have to be patient with Mother Nature."

"Mother Nature!" mimicked the man, throwing his arms into the air. "I can't wait around for Mother Nature. I get paid for making decisions and it's damn disconcerting to run into a bunch of people who can't make things happen." Angry, he turned back to the petite young agent and asked, "Have you exhausted *all* avenues getting me into Medford tonight?"

Drawing in a deep breath and then exhaling heavily, the harassed agent said patiently, "You know, perhaps we haven't 'exhausted' all our sources of help. I think I know someone who can be of assistance." She stepped from behind her counter and walked to the big bay window overlooking the mass of grounded planes on the runway. With both hands flat against the large pane of glass, she leaned her small body against it and looked out into the vast blackness of the late night now veiled in a thick white mist of dense fog. Turning her head heavenward, in a sweet and melodic tone she gently pleaded, "God, I've been unable to help this poor, frustrated man. Could you please clear out this fog so this important guy can get to his destination?"

The crowd clapped and cheered, applauding her actions. With that, the diminutive and uniform-clad young woman stepped back behind her counter, picked up the microphone and looked into the crowd, "Would anyone else with the expectation that God will clear this ground fog, and pronto, please make a line behind the distinguished gentleman to my right. Anyone else who would like to make alternative arrangements for early morning flights, please form a line to the left.

"For anyone interested in driving to the nearby cities, there are seven rental car agencies with approximately 65 total cars left on the lots. For those wishing to get a hotel room for the night, there is a listing of all hotels located nearby right next to the baggage-claim area. I will tell you it's my experience that during this particular season, it's not uncommon for the 6:55 and 8:00 A.M. morning flights in such weather conditions to depart later than usual. That was true this morning, as it was for several mornings these past two weeks. For those who may want to forewarn family, friends and business associates in case that happens, there are additional phones in each of the adjacent wings of this terminal. I'm sorry for the canceled flights. There's really no way of knowing ahead of time that a flight will be canceled. Sometimes the fog sets in and clears out in a matter of minutes. Sometimes it lingers for a few hours at a time. There just isn't much I can do about it, except to be as efficient as I can in helping you sort out the best way to get you to your next destination."

Turning in the direction of the now bewildered business-man, she continued, "Though I am obliged to be the recipient of your stress and to cushion it to the best of my ability, my absorbing it won't do any of us much good. I really am very sorry for your inconvenience, but I would rather spend my time resolving our plight—effectively."

Turning back to the rest of us, she continued, "I'll do my very best to help each and every one of you sort out your alternatives." She lay down the hand PA system amplifying her lovely voice and returned to her place in front of the computer. Looking at the next traveler in line, she asked sweetly, "May I help you, sir?"

Bewildered that his uncomely outburst hadn't yielded results that coincided with *his* dictates, the businessman— still clinging to his self-righteous dignity—stormed away in the direction of the telephones, his mighty briefcase swinging with each kingly stride.

So we three stranded strangers, all fellow travelers in the night trying to get to a town some miles away, began our journey to the rental car window.

It was a trip I will not soon forget. During that four-and-a-half-hour ride, the three of us talked about our work and our families and shared a sense of how we viewed life in general. We were, quite frankly, amazed at the synergy we shared and the enormous enjoyment we found in each other's company. The time seemed to quickly evaporate. As the trip neared its end, we all knew that we wanted to stay in touch. We gladly exchanged business cards, adding our home phone numbers beside the perfunctory printed ones.

And stay in touch we did. As it turned out, Bill was in the seminar business and Jerry worked for a publishing house. Since meeting Bill, I have spoken on a number of occasions to groups he assembled. Two years to the very date of the memorable evening, I signed a book contract with Jerry's publishing house for my book, *Keeping Our Children Safe: A Guide to Physical, Emotional, Spiritual & Intellectual Wellness.*

While connections with these two men turned out to be enormously successful for me in terms of business, I place much greater value on what has happened as a result of our connection on a personal level. Both of these men are extraordinarily personable people. They are thoughtful and caring; they honor the power of connection with family, friends and even strangers. These qualities were instrumental in forming the bond of friendship we share.

Each of us now knows something of the others' lives and families and has on occasion called upon each other to share a family joy and victory or to help in a matter of concern. Once, one of the men asked me for guidance in repairing the rift between him and his son and assistance in helping him seek out a drug treatment program for his son. Several years later, when his child had mended his health and returned to his goals, I was honored to help the young man get accepted to a university where I serve on the board of trustees. The other gentlemen once called on me to be part of a prayer chain for a dear friend of his. From time-to-time he'll call and ask if he can fax me copy he'd like me to edit or on which he'd like me to provide constructive feedback.

It's been said that God moves in mysterious ways. Perhaps fog is one of them. After all, thoughts of fog often evoke images of something hidden—something very much like God's movements in generating these circumstances of our lives.

It has also been said that there are no mistakes, that all things happen for a reason and eventually for a good outcome. Like the fog, perhaps these events are controlled by someone bigger and more important than us—someone who has bigger plans for us—for our lives and its details—than those we are capable of generating for ourselves. Certainly, such a plan unfolded for us that evening.

5

About That Flower...

You will find as you look back upon your life,
that the moments that stand out, the moments you have
really lived, are the moments when you have
done things in the spirit of love.

—Henry Drummond

She always wore a flower in her hair. Always. Mostly I thought it looked strange. A flower in midday? To work? To professional meetings?

She was an aspiring graphic designer in the large, busy office where I worked. Every day she sailed into the office with its ultramodern crisp decor wearing a flower in her shoulder-length hair. Usually color-coordinated with her otherwise suitable attire, the flower bloomed as a small parasol of vivid color, opened on a large backdrop of dark brunette waves. There were times, like at the company Christmas party, where the flower added a touch of festivity and seemed appropriate. At work, however, it just seemed out of place.

Some of the more "professionally minded" women in the office were practically indignant about it. They thought someone ought to take her aside and inform her of the "rules" for being "taken seriously" in the business world. Others among us, myself included, thought it just an odd quirk and privately referred to her as "flower-power" or "girl-flower."

"Has 'flower-power' completed the preliminary design on the new brochure?" one of us would ask the other with a lopsided smile.

"Of course. It turned out great—her work has really blossomed," might be the reply. Housed in patronizing smiles of shared amusement, our mockery seemed innocent to us.

To my knowledge no one questioned the young woman as to why a flower accompanied her to work each day. In fact, we probably would have been more inclined to question her had she shown up without it.

One day she did. When she delivered a project to my office, I queried her about the missing flower. "I noticed there is no flower in your hair today," I said casually. "I'm so used to seeing you wear one that it almost seems as if something is missing."

"Oh, yes," she replied quietly, in a rather somber tone. This was a departure from her usual bright and perky personality. A pregnant pause followed, prompting me to ask, "Are you okay?" Though I was hoping for a "Yes, I'm fine" response, intuitively I knew I had treaded on something bigger than a missing flower.

"Oh," she said softly, with an expression encumbered with recollection and sorrow. "Today is the anniversary of my mother's death. I miss her so much. I guess I'm a bit blue."

"I understand," I said, feeling compassion for her but not wanting to wade into her emotional waters. "I'm sure it's very difficult for you to talk about," I continued, the business part of me hoping that she would agree. My heart, however, truly understood that there was more.

"No. It's okay, really. I know that I'm extraordinarily sensitive today. This is a day of mourning, I suppose. You see, my mother knew that she was losing her life to cancer. Eventually, she died. I was 15 at the time. We were very close. She was so loving, so giving. Because she knew she was dying she prerecorded individual birthday messages. I was to watch one every year on my birthday, from age 16 until I reached 25. Today is my 25th birthday, and this morning I watched the video she prepared for this day. I guess I'm still digesting it . . . and so wishing my mother was alive."

"My heart goes out to you," I said.

"Thank you for your kindness," she said smiling sadly. "Oh, and the missing flower you asked about? When I was a little girl, my mother often put flowers in my hair. One day when she was in the hospital, I took her this beautiful rose from her garden. As I held it up to her so she could smell it, she took the lovely flower from me, pulled me close to her and, stroking my hair and brushing it away from my face—in the exact manner she did when I was a little girl—she placed the flower in my hair, just as she had done so many times . . ." She paused and, as tears clouded her eyes, added sadly, "Mom died later that day. I've worn a flower in my hair since—it made me feel as though she were with me, if only in spirit."

To keep from crying aloud, she sighed deeply before continuing. "Today, as I watched the video designed for me on this birthday, my mother said she was sorry for not being able to be there for me as I grew up. She said she hoped she had been a good parent and asked for a *sign* that I was becoming 'self-sufficient.' That's the way my mother thought—the way she talked." She looked at me, smiling fondly at the memory.

"What a very loving and touching living memory," I said sincerely.

"Yes," she agreed nodding her head. "So I thought, a *sign*, what could I do to communicate that I had learned to be self-reliant? It seemed it was the flower that had to go. But I'll miss it and what it represents."

As if momentarily transported to a memory that held much strength and dignity, her melancholy eyes transformed into a gaze that was both serene and brave. "I am so lucky to have her . . ." she said. Her eyes met mine again. Intuitively trusting what she saw there, she pressed a tissue softly against her eyes and unapologetically allowed herself to shed her sadness with tears.

Her strength refortified, she said, "I don't need to wear a flower to be reminded of these things. I really do know that. The flower was just an outward sign of my treasured memories. Mom left a legacy rich in love and it will take more than an absent flower to dim its presence. Time can never take away her gift of love—nor diminish the manner in which she shared it." Her voice trailed off again before finally saying, "Still, I will miss it . . ."

She sighed a deep breath and, changing emotional gears, shifted from her private self into her professional self. Assertively she said, "Oh, here's the project. I hope it meets with your approval." She handed me the neatly prepared folder, signed with a hand-drawn flower—her signature trademark—below her name.

When I was young girl, my mother used the phrase, "Never judge another person until you've walked a mile in her shoes." I thought about all the times I was insensitive to this young woman with the flower in her hair. I was disappointed in myself that I had done this in the absence of information, not knowing the young woman's fate and the cross that was hers to bear. That day I knew that the flower this young woman wore in her hair was symbolic of her outpouring of love—a way for her to stay connected to the mother she had lost.

I looked over the project she had completed and felt honored that it had been treated by one with such depth and capacity for *feeling* . . . of *being*. It was with respect and esteem that I now saw clearly the enormity of her ability to bring the past into the future, integrating it as a way to give meaning to the present.

No wonder her work was consistently excellent. She lived in her heart daily.

And caused me to revisit mine.

6

Equal Pay for Equal Worth

*Like a rare virus, wisdom tends to
break out at unexpected times, and it's mostly people
with compassion and understanding
who are susceptible to it.*

—Alan Alda

"What do I owe you, John?" my dad asked the first young man he had hired to help put up the last of the season's hay.

"That'll be $55, Mr. Burres," John said. Dad wrote him a check for $55. "Thank you for your work, John," my father said respectfully.

"What do I owe you, Michael?" my father asked the second young man who had worked the same number of hours as John.

"You owe me $75," Michael said.

With a look of surprise, my dad asked quietly, "How do you figure that, Michael?"

"Oh," said Michael, "I charge from the time I get into my car to drive to the job site, until the time I get back home, plus gas mileage and meal allowance."

"I see," said my dad, writing him a check for $75.

"And what about you, Nathan?" Dad inquired. "What do I owe you?"

"You owe me $38.50, Mr. Burres," Nathan said.

Again my father was surprised at the discrepancy in the amount requested. The third young man, like the other two, had been hired for the same job and had put in equal time (and had come from the same small town just a couple of miles away). My father asked for clarification.

"How did you arrive at that figure, Nathan?"

"Well," said Nathan, "I didn't charge you for the lunch break since your wife prepared and served lunch. There were several times when I had to wait around until the next load of hay was hauled in from the field in order to put it into the loft. I didn't have gas expenses since I came with my buddies. So the actual number of hours worked brings my pay to $38.50."

My father wrote him out a check for $100.

Dad then looked at the three young men—stricken silent by my father's actions—all of whom were a bit bewildered by the differing amounts on their individual checks.

"I always pay a man his *worth*, boys. Where I come from we call that equal pay for equal worth."

He looked benevolently at the three young men before him and in his typical fatherly style added, "I like to see a man bring his heart to work."

7

Margaret

*Feeling unloved is the
worst poverty in the world.*

—Mother Teresa

I was attending a four-day California Teen Talent competition with my daughter in a small city on the northern California coastline. On the third day, a special afternoon and evening was planned just for the hundred-plus young people in this event so we parents were on our own. Several of us asked the concierge where we might have an informal dinner at an outdoor cafe. We were directed to "restaurant row" where a particular bistro was recommended.

When I arrived at the restaurant's parking lot, I was informed that it was full and I had to park elsewhere—nearly half a mile away, as it turned out. Taking a shortcut on the walk back, I crossed through the parking lot that was supposedly full and noticed a badly dented, very dirty, baby-blue old-model Cadillac carelessly parked lengthwise and taking up several parking spaces. It was a peculiar sight and upsetting, too. How could anyone be so thoughtless?

Nearing the vehicle, I noticed a large-skulled German shepherd sitting in the back seat investigating my every move. The window was down, the animal's ears were up and his teeth were bared. The shiver on the back of my neck was a tip-off that caution was warranted. My instincts were correct. By the time my next step touched ground, the agitated hound was on all fours, his body pressed tight against the window frame. With each step I took, the dog issued a low-grade guttural snarl reverberating with impending danger. My fear mounting, I side-stepped to allow several more feet of space between the car and me. It was from this vantage point that I noticed a docile kitten sitting alongside this menacing canine, not at all fearful of this big, snarling beast. Then I noticed another oddity—an enormous dark-haired woman sitting in the driver's seat, crocheting.

The sight of this obese, crocheting woman and her odd menagerie of animals intensified my curiosity about this flagrantly parked car (in what should have been my parking space). I continued examining this situation. Even an ample drink of these incongruous images couldn't pour out a logical explanation. There was more to come: as I drew closer, even more bizarre images met my eyes. The car was packed chock-full of clothes, as if someone had stuffed it with armfuls of laundry. Door to door, dashboard to the back window, the clothes were packed in solid. The animals couldn't help but tread on them. It was an amazing sight.

I was still gawking when the woman glanced up from her crocheting. In the most lovely songbird voice, she chirped merrily, "Hi! Is this a lovely evening, or what!" These words danced from a shapely and unpainted mouth with a more-than-generous smile. Her hazel-colored eyes sparkled with zest, zeal and friendliness. It was hard to tell, but she looked about 35 or 40. At the sound of her voice, the dog relaxed and sat down. His original aggression was now transformed by a newfound feeling of friendship and a longing to be petted. This stimulated a pant-and-drool routine that caused a constant stream of slobber to drip from the tip of his long tongue and from small crevices in his enormous jowls.

The woman's neighborly demeanor and invitation to talk persuaded me to share a moment. I badly wanted to ask, "How on earth can you tolerate this mess?" and, "How long have you been sitting here?" I wondered if maybe she had arrived early and this was her way of reserving parking spaces for others joining her for dinner. Instead, I replied less than enthusiastically, "Yes, this is a beautiful evening. Are you waiting to join friends to have dinner in one of the restaurants here?"

"Oh, noooooooo!" she said, drawling the "no" for emphasis. "I don't have any friends. I'll just be here in the car." Although her response was dismaying, she sounded content.

"How long have you been in your car?" I asked, trying to divert my stare from her remarkable disarrangement. I chose to ignore her insensate statement about not having friends; everyone has some sort of friends—it's just a question of caliber.

"By the way, my name is Margaret," she declared. Then with the same bright smile she used when we first met, she answered my question by saying, "This ol' car has been my home for just about two years now."

I thought she didn't understand me. "It looks like you've been sitting there for some time!" I said, hoping my expression didn't reveal the righteous indignation I felt.

"Well, I have been here a pretty long time!" Margaret assured me. "I live in here."

"Really? You live in the car?" I asked, glancing at her very oily and uncombed hair. Then, as politely as I could, I stammered, "Well, what do you do when you want to shower?"

"Oh," Margaret replied sweetly, "I simply go over there." Her crochet hook in hand, she pointed in the direction of the Best Western hotel. Without my prompting her to explain, she elaborated, "I take the elevator up to the second floor, sit in the lounge area there and watch for guests leaving with their luggage. Then, as politely as I can, I ask if I might use the shower facilities."

"Well, that's certainly innovative!" I said, thinking that her problem-solving skills surpassed some of the best managers I'd worked with over the years. Wondering whether hotel guests might grant such a bold request, I questioned, "Does that always work for you?"

Her head instantly turned in my direction as she looked me in the eyes to see if the question was sincere or mocking. "Well, of course not!" she replied, sounding shocked that I should be so naive as to believe that it would always yield a "yes" response. "You can imagine why some people might say no. You see," she said, punctuating her thought with a big sigh as she looked me over, "when a guest arrives at the hotel, an imprint is taken of their credit card. Depending on whether the card is silver, gold or platinum edition . . ." I must have met her litmus test, because Margaret proceeded to dole out a lesson in credit card billing cycles. She concluded my education by saying, "So, you can understand why some cardholders worry that I might use the room phone and charge up a bill or, worse, stay the afternoon and they'd be charged for another day. No, I don't always get a thumbs-up, but sometimes I do!" She sounded rather pleased with her success rate.

The incongruence was becoming ever more incomprehensible. Clearly Margaret was an intelligent woman, eloquently articulate and in command of an elegant vocabulary. She was also friendly and outgoing and, perhaps, she knew something about credit card billing cycles that I didn't. My curiosity prompted me to press on. "Why do you live in your car?" I asked.

At this question, her voice lost its confident tone and she hung her head. "Well, it's like this," she began, her head lowering even more and her voice taking on a lamenting tone, "my boss fired me. Then my husband left me." She paused and stared straight ahead, perhaps wondering if she should reveal all this to a perfect stranger. "Oh well," she continued, as if it didn't matter, "everyone *knew* I'd never amount to much. My father said I'd never get it together and I guess he was right. 'Margaret,' he criticized, 'You'll end up a bum, or marry one.' And I did. I married a bum, an alcoholic bum, like my dad. And like my dad, he used to remind me daily that I was nothing special. Guess I am what they said." She now sounded more sad than remorseful.

I tried to picture her as a young girl, sitting at her desk at school or engaged in conversation at the dinner table with her sister and parents. "What about your mother?" I asked. "Surely she thought you were special." In a most sarcastic tone, Margaret replied, "In *my* family, my father *controlled* all the other voices, *his* opinion mattered most. Unfortunately, he didn't have anything good to say, or worth saying, for that matter." Just as quickly as the sarcasm had entered her voice, it left, replaced by a tone of melancholy. She now looked sad, too, as if wounded anew by the hurtful words echoed so long ago in her childhood. It was easy to see that this memory caused her pain. I felt for her. Caring, I asked, "Margaret, isn't there *anyone* in your family you can turn to?"

Looking forlorn, she said *no* by shaking her head slowly from side to side, then accused her sister of adding to the let-downs. "My sister lives across town. But she wouldn't give me money. If she had, I might not have to live out of my car." In an unconvincing attempt to stimulate pity, she looked at me from the corner of her eyes but knew right away I wasn't buying into it. Instantly she dropped the "poor me" attitude, laughed and said, "Well, she has every right to be embarrassed by me, doesn't she?"

I realized we were back to square one. Wanting to break the saga of how everyone had done her in, I commented, "Well, surely there's some place where you can get help. A halfway house perhaps?"

"Are you kidding?" she shrieked, waving her crochet needle at me for emphasis. "This town has those kinds of places for men but not for women." It was obvious that now she was blaming her gender for her victimization.

I was beginning to understand that she had been derailed by a lifelong series of negative events, so I tried to steer her onto another track. Seeing the colorful, crocheted doilies stacked on the dashboard and the colorful knitted afghan wrapped around her shoulders, I asked enthusiastically, "The afghan you're wearing is beautiful. Did you knit it?"

"Yup," she said, dead-ending the conversation.

Attempting to prod her on, I asked, "Do you take your knitted and crocheted pieces to stores to sell them on consignment?" I figured she had to make money somehow. As far as I could tell, Margaret didn't appear to be destitute.

Her scowl intensified. "Nah," she drawled. "Who would want these worthless things?"

I was about to give up but decided to try one more time. "Is there something you want more than anything else, Margaret, a *goal* of some kind?"

Her eyes lit up with longing. "Oh, that's easy! I want to be able to take a bath in my own tub, any time I want, without having to ask anyone's permission. I'd like to have a place of my own!"

My spirits soared. Now we were getting somewhere! "Well, then," I asked cheerfully, "if I come here next year, where will I find you? Where will you be?"

"Why, right here!" she said, smiling sweetly. "I'm not going anywhere." She looked sincere.

I believed her—and excused myself for dinner.

At dinner we parents joyously talked about our children's accomplishments and how proud we were that they were healthy, bright and talented, and so enthusiastically engaged in their lives. But I couldn't get Margaret off my mind. The thought of Margaret as a little girl who didn't get all the love and hugs she needed was an unsettling thought. Like our children, Margaret was not without talent, aptitude and interpersonal skills. Why *couldn't* she transform her life? Why *wouldn't* she? Had the scars caused by not enough loving and acceptance from those who mattered most blocked the arteries to her heart? Worse, had it prevented her from loving herself? Why hadn't she reached her goal of having a place of her own? Had the messages that contributed to her low self-esteem been played over and over for so long that she now believed them and had given up wanting to forge ahead? How could such a friendly, communicative, intelligent woman not possess the ability to jump-start her life, to start over? No one's life is without trials, not even these high-spirited, high self-esteem young people—the best of the best in their schools throughout the state. Here they were, all gathered in this little town, cooperatively showcasing their talents and achievements. These children were not sitting in someone else's parking space.

And Margaret still was.

I left the restaurant nearly two hours later. Passing through the parking lot, I once again encountered Margaret. She was no longer crocheting but held a book in one hand and a flashlight in the other. As I approached, she glanced up. In a sweet and rather somber voice, she said demurely, "Thank you for taking the time to talk with me earlier. I know you probably think that I'm just a homeless woman, but I'm a good person. I really am."

"I'm sure you are, Margaret," I said sensitively.

"You probably think that I'm just a lazy, irresponsible person . . ." she continued. I could tell that she was trying to get me to linger for a moment and that she was well aware that I really didn't want to.

"No," I said, smiling sympathetically but not really wanting to confirm her own low self-regard. "I just see a friendly, intelligent woman who has had a few setbacks and needs some time to regroup."

Without pretense or defense, Margaret concurred. "You're right. Here I sit with a couple of years of college, I once had a job, a marriage—all the things most people would want—but the 'good life' has eluded me. You may not believe it, but I once went to dinner with friends here in these very restaurants, like you did tonight." She sighed and shook her head in disgust and self-loathing.

Phrasing my words carefully, I said slowly, "Margaret, I understand what it's like to feel trapped in your own circumstances, but do you feel it's your choice to be here now?"

"Oh sure," she readily agreed once more. "I'm as guilty as anyone for making my own life miserable."

I was amazed at her candor and realized that she was even more emotionally literate than I had earlier assessed. Perhaps she no longer wanted to be a bystander in her life. Looking down at her lap, she asked, "Tell me, when you saw me earlier this evening, what was the first thing that came to your mind?"

"Well, to tell you the truth, I wanted your parking space!" I said bluntly.

Entirely unrepentant, Margaret tossed her head back and laughed. "I thought as much!" she declared, obviously amused by my candid response. "But after that," I added, perhaps feeling justified by what I perceived as her ability to handle my honesty, "my heart ached for you because you obviously felt unwanted, uncared for and forgotten by everybody." Her jovial facade came down and I could see the lost and lonely woman beneath. Her expression then transformed into one of relief, perhaps grateful that someone else understood how she felt.

Margaret nodded amiably, then frowned. "Do you believe this notion that we become what we believe about ourselves?" she questioned.

"Yes," I said with conviction. "I do believe that we can think about what we really want for ourselves and then make the decision to stay on track toward our goals. Determination is a large part of bringing our goals to fruition. Of course it helps if in childhood we've been scripted to believe in ourselves. I do think the message about self-worth begins there. But even so, as an adult, you have to decide that your own opinion of yourself counts. Now it's your vote about who you are and what you want to be and do—what you want to bring about in your life—that matters most. It's an important vote—feelings of self-worth are played out in our actions."

"How so?" she asked with obvious interest.

"Self-worth acts as a price tag," I said.

"A price tag?" she questioned.

"We can choose to believe we're valuable goods or we can believe we're mark-downs," I explained. "Maybe you've heard the little story about a young boy who came home crying because a classmate called him a sissy?" Her eyes bright and attentive, she signaled with a slight nod that I should continue.

"'Why are you crying?' his Grandma asked. 'Because Paul called me a sissy. Do you think I'm a sissy, Grandma?'

"'Oh no,' said the grandmother. 'I think you're a Ferrari.'

"'What?' said the boy, trying to make sense of what his grandmother had said. 'Why do you think I'm a car?'

"'Well, if you believe that because Paul called you a sissy you are, you might as well believe you're a car, and while you're at it, a great one at that. Why be a sissy when you can be a Ferrari?'

"'Oh,' exclaimed the boy gleefully, feeling quite relieved. 'I get to decide what I am!'

"That applies to us all, Margaret. Why be a sissy when you can be a Ferrari?"

"Do you believe our thoughts are that powerful?" she quizzed.

My words tinged with urgency, "Oh, Margaret," I said, softly, now thinking of her more as a sister on the journey rather than a person sleepwalking in her life. "I think that both words and actions really do influence us, especially when we are young. Though the message you were given while growing up was destructive to your self-esteem, now you have to make the choice to either believe in yourself and your ability to create the life you want, or to remain a victim of circumstance and excuse yourself from responsibility. Does that make sense to you, Margaret?" I asked, hoping she heard these words as coming from my heart and not as a lecture.

"To tell you the truth," Margaret replied, "I'm a bit tired of being the diva of the delayed, rescheduled, bumped and burned out. But I have no one in my life. I'm so alone. I have no one to help me. No one to love." Tears flooded her eyes as she added, *"I don't even love me."*

"Oh, Margaret," I said softly. "I understand the feeling. Sometimes the courage to overcome may be granted by someone else reaching out to love us and to help us find our way back, but all too often it's our own task to do for ourselves. Self-acceptance is largely your work to do *with* and *for* yourself. But you have to care enough about yourself to want to try it." Again I hoped that she wouldn't think this was a lecture. I added gently, "Just by the things you've said, I see such a good and decent person who has so much to offer and so much happiness left to live, if only you'll believe that you can and you make an effort to go after what you really want." I paused and looked her deeply in the eyes before adding, "Don't you think you can?" Margaret considered my question. Our eyes held a steady, respectful and mutually caring gaze. Finally she answered, "I don't know, do *you* think I can?"

"Yes, I do, but that's not what matters," I said. She searched my face intently, perhaps for any hint I might be patronizing her. Satisfied I wasn't, she exuberantly ordered, "Then ask me again where I'll be when you come here next year!"

"Okay," I said, laughing. "Margaret, when I come here again next year, where shall I find you?" Laughing like a schoolgirl, she announced, "This Ferrari's going to be in a place of my own! And you can have this parking space!"

"Deal," I said, thrusting my hand out to her.

"It's a deal, then!" Margaret said, grabbing my hand and shaking it vigorously.

Once again looking me directly in the eyes, she said softly and sincerely, "Thank you so much for taking the time to talk with me. You don't know how much it meant."

"The pleasure is mine, Margaret," I said. "I'll be rooting for you. I know *you* can do it. I believe in you."

"Wow," she said softly, making no attempt to stop the tears trickling down her checks. Now absorbed in her own thoughts, she nodded her head slowly up and down, as if reassuring herself, or perhaps she was busy scripting a list of commitments and promises.

More to herself than to me, she softly murmured, "It's time I start believing in me, too."

8

Serving You Well

The Lord is close to the brokenhearted.

—Psalms 34:18

Anna picked up John's left hand, now folded across his chest—placed it in hers—and gently stroked it. Slowly the fingers of her frail hand tenderly traced the outline of his weathered hand, as if to memorize the feel of it. She closed her eyes, as if remembering this sensation and locking it away deep in her heart where she would never forget it. She then opened her eyes and touched each of his fingers.

When she came to the thick gold wedding band, she paused as though remembering other times. She leaned down and gently gave the hand one last parting kiss. "I hope I have served you well, my love," she whispered. These words were not about subservience, but rather the strength, compassion and devotion she freely offered and the knowledge of what her love had truly meant in his life, and his in hers.

They adored each other during 40 years of married life. Now he was gone. They were a couple bonded together by time and experiences shared, and a promise to honor their commitment in good times, bad times, all times. "Soulmates," they had called themselves.

She believed in her heart that there must be a heaven. There, somehow, she would reunite with the spirit of the man she had loved so deeply throughout her life. The man whose body, whose shell, now lay empty and lifeless before her.

Witnessing this quiet good-bye, I could only imagine the intense feelings of loss she was experiencing. Yet, she seemed comforted by her own inner strength and belief. With tear-filled eyes and a sweet and peaceful face, she turned and moved from her husband's casket.

Serving, service. What a precious and honorable gift of the heart.

9

Leaving Room for Angels

Honor the wisdom of the heart.

—Emmanuel

Staring wide-eyed and open-mouthed at the clerk at the dry cleaners, I repeated, "Come back this afternoon?" Annoyed, I badgered, "When I brought my suit in on Monday, I specifically asked that it be ready for me by noon, and I was assured it would. I've got to have it for a business trip; my flight leaves *very* early in the morning. I've got a million and one things to do . . ." My mind quickly reviewed my to-do list, reminding me of the back-to-back appointments I'd scheduled at my office. "I just don't have the *time* for another trip back here this afternoon," I moaned.

The clerk's eyes conveyed a sincere "wish-I-could-help" sympathy. She apologized, then assured me, "If you can come back in a couple hours, I'll personally make sure that it's ready for you."

I looked at my watch and grumbled on my way out, "Another trip back here this afternoon is the one thing I don't need!" My anxiety growing like some oversized creature in a science fiction movie, I dashed out the door in high gear, nearly crashing into a young woman cautiously pushing a baby stroller down the sidewalk. In leaping out of *her* way, I nearly bumped into two young lovers, arm-in-arm, strolling leisurely down the street in front of me. I had no more recovered from side-stepping the two of them when I noticed the two middle-aged businessmen patiently waiting for the light to turn to green so they could cross the street. Obviously noticing I was in a hurry, in unison they signaled for me to proceed in front of them.

Everyone it seemed, had ample *time*. Too many things to do and never enough time to do them in, I was forever juggling a dozen projects, errands and roles at once. From coordinating the many activities in my own life and those of my family to upholding the many responsibilities in my work world, time was always at a premium. I always had nine irons in the fire. When others said, "Take time to smell the roses," I had no idea what they were talking about.

Time was one thing I never had enough of.

Time. What a precious commodity. It is, perhaps, the

greatest collateral we have as leverage. The amount of time we share with others is often added up, the total score used to equate exactly how much value we've assigned them. My teenager's "best" friend was that person with whom she shared hours upon hours of uncensored time. Lovers take the time to linger in unhurried moments. "Giving time" is a positive gesture; "withholding time," a negative. When my daughter was little, discipline meant "time out," time away from the people and rooms she loved the most. In my business world, the more value or worth a client or employee was perceived as having, the more of my time they were granted. On the other side of this, I withheld time from those who took advantage or infringed upon my good nature.

Time. How I wished I had more of it. Oh, the luxury of that young mother's schedule, or those lovers, or those businessmen. I said out loud, "That's exactly what I want for Christmas, a day of boredom! In the meantime," I muttered, turning my eyes heavenward, "I'd settle for a few hours when time stands still."

Just as I was saying this—still walking a mile a minute to get back to my car and resume the countdown on my lengthy errand list—my quick pace was abruptly brought to a halt. In front of me was a *very* tiny and *very, very* old man, standing right in the middle of the sidewalk. He was dressed in brown corduroy pants and a brown tweed jacket complete with a gray wool vest with knobby leather-covered buttons. He wore a gray and red plaid neck scarf wrapped haphazardly around his neck. With one hand he held it tightly in place, with the other, he clutched a well-worn cane made of dark wood. Nearly toe-to-toe now, I looked at him more closely: a hearing aid was tucked in each of his petite, elfin-shaped ears, and he sported a crinkled blue fisherman's hat—complete with metal Shriner's pin and a perky little, puffy, pink and gray feather—on top of his small round head. Peering into his rheumy eyes, I noted that the poor little man looked bewildered. What I didn't know was that he was totally *lost.*

Though it took some effort on his part to focus in on me, eventually he did. The look on his face was one of sheer panic. Slowly he opened his tiny oval mouth and stuttered something completely inaudible. Still in motion, I assumed he would move out of my way. He wasn't making much progress in deciding what to do. At first I thought it was my speed and haste that alarmed him, but on second thought I realized he hadn't seen or heard me coming. The problem was that he stood blocking my path, unable to make up his mind which way to move in order to get out of my way. Dazed as he seemed to be, he did a clumsy two-step with me, stiffly tottering back and forth while I tried to maneuver my way past him.

Make your move, little man, I thought. *I'm in a big hurry and you could get run over here! Just exactly* which *way are you going?* He seemed incapable of reaching any conclusion. Relieving him of that responsibility, I zipped around him, barreling on my way.

I hadn't proceeded 10 feet when my heart fluttered the message, *Stop! He needs your help.* It was as if I had walked into an invisible brick wall. Almost involuntarily, I found myself turning to the man. A look of alarm and panic washed across his face. An association from out of the past brought into clear view a vivid picture of my daughter. "Mommy," my little girl would call to me, "there's the angel again! I can feel her." Inevitably, her tiny hand zoomed to her chest as she said, "She's playing in my heart, Mommy!" A coquettish little creature, these words were said at those times when she felt especially joyful, gleeful, filled with goodness, giggles and laughter. Though I didn't really know exactly where this phrase originated for her, I never tired of hearing her say it, especially since the common denominator that triggered her words was *kindness*.

This seemed to be exactly what this moment called for. Exchanging my Type A for a dose of kindness, I turned back to the little old man. The baffled look on his face, just now registering that perhaps I had intended to pass him by, was one of entreaty. His expression had changed from scared to urgent.

It was a defining moment. Slowly, I walked back to him.

"Do you need directions?" I asked.

He just stared at me blankly. "Do you need directions?" I repeated a bit louder.

This time he appeared to be carefully considering my question, slowly closing his wrinkled eyes as if to envision when the planets would be in alignment. "Nnnnnnn," he murmured. "Nnnnnnn." With great effort he lifted the small, withered and badly gnarled fingers of his left hand about waist high and waved listlessly, pointing down the street. I decided he meant "North."

"North is that way," I said, pointing in the opposite direction. Slowly he shook his head and once again uttered, "Nnnnnnn."

Wow, I thought. *I'm in a hurry and now I've gotten myself into a situation of helping this person who needs to be somewhere, but* where? *On top of it all, he can't even communicate.* I looked at my watch, drew a deep breath and tried again.

"Do you need directions?" I asked slowly, enunciating my words clearly and watching as he carefully watched my lips to see what words were forming there. Without answering me, he pointed in the direction of the phone booth ahead. *He's unfamiliar with this area,* I thought. *Perhaps a stroke left him without language and unable to communicate in words, making his predicament all the more frightening to him and difficult for me.* I looked in the direction of the phone booth. *That's a great idea,* I thought. *I'll walk with him to the phone booth, hand him the telephone book and let him show me his address. Then, I'll call a cab to get him home or take him there myself.* I put my hand under his right elbow in an effort to move in the direction of the phone booth only to discover that the poor little guy couldn't do much more than shuffle!

It took a full 20 minutes for the two of us to move little more than 10 feet!

Once at the phone booth, he refused to look at the phone book. *Oh great Scott!* I thought. *Now what? What's he trying to tell me? Where does he live? Who does he belong to? Should I just leave him here? He made his way here, surely he would make it to wherever he was going.* His steadfast cane held all his weight as he leaned on it, his full concentration required to maintain his balance and not fall to the ground. Okay, so he wouldn't make it to wherever he was going. I looked around at the busy intersection, then back at him with his obvious incoherence. I couldn't just leave him here. I would have to find *someone* who knew him. *Who?* I looked around. No one in sight looked as though they had lost their great-great-grandfather! I would have to take him *somewhere*. *Where?*

Searching his face again, I carefully enunciated, "Where do you live?"

This time, he replied, "Tank you," and reached to shake my hand, or so I thought. Instead, he reached beyond my grasp and pointed in the direction of the street.

"This way? You live this way? We should go this way?" I inquired. Desperate for some sort of direction, I took the movements of his head as agreement.

At tortoise speed, we started "shuffling" in the direction of "down the street." As we hobbled along, step by tiny labored step, I searched the passing faces for anyone who might be looking for him, or even knew him, or knew of his circumstance, where he might live or who might be in charge of his care.

"Excuse me," I asked several passersby, "Do you by any chance know this gentleman? Or know where he lives?" My inquiries were usually met by brusque "no's" or silent negative shakes of the head, as people zoomed about their business. I did receive an occasional apology of, "I'm sorry I can't help you."

I was familiar with Drake University, which was right across the street, so I decided to try taking him to the security office on campus. During the course of that journey, I looked at my watch and noticed that nearly 45 minutes of precious —and limited— time had ticked away. Retrieving the cellular phone I carried in my purse, I called my office.

"Tina," I said in my best Arnold Schwarzenegger voice, "I'll be back! But late! I'm on the Drake University campus, taking a lost elderly gentlemen to the security office. We're moving *very* slowly, but I'm confident we'll be there any day now! Please try to move my first appointment to the end of the day."

Chuckling, she said, "That's funny! I can't quite picture you doing anything *slowly*. I'm surprised that by now you haven't just dragged him back to the office with you. It'd take less time—and we can always use an extra pair of hands around this place." She was right, this was a funny scene—or at least peculiar—but what else could I do? "And by the way," Tina went on, "the appointment with Mr. Bankus is canceled. He called and said he was going to get out of the office early today. With the day being so beautiful, he said he wanted to take some time to enjoy the outdoors. Maybe you'll get a chance to enjoy it, too—walking *slowly* to the security office."

She was right. Though my mind and movements raced a mile a minute, there was nothing I could do now but slow my inner world down to match this outer reality.

It's amazing how different the world looks when you slow down from 80 mph to 20 mph. It's sort of like going from racing a Jaguar at the Camel Grand Prix to riding a bicycle for two in the park. It's a real paradigm shift: without the blur of speed, every sight seems clearer.

I discovered an amazingly different world in those moments of seemingly suspended time. Ambling slowly along with the little man's arm linked compliantly with mine, I looked down and observed itty-bitty white and purple flowers had pushed themselves up through the bright green carpet of grass. Here the dainty, fragile flowers bloomed in all their splendor, without caring that passersby would have to look oh-so-closely in order to see them in the first place, much less appreciate their delicate beauty.

Brown-spectacled squirrels with lush bushy tails dashed from tree trunk to tree trunk. Without missing so much as a single sound or flicker, they stopped their frenzied scurry just long enough to make a judgment as to whether or not they should be concerned. Their heads were in constant up-and-down and side-to-side motion as they scrutinized the sounds of people near and far. Their alert faces registered occasional alarm as they attended to their chores of searching out and retrieving the acorns in the thickly padded grass.

Even the birds seemed joyful, happily basking in the warm glow of the fall season's sun and gentle breeze the day offered. Perched in the lush treetops nearby, they chirped about their happiness, their chorus sweetly adding to this perfect day.

I looked up and surveyed the sky. The blue of certain striking eyes, it held the drifting forms of those rounded creatures of my childhood, the ones I saw while lying on a lawn, hidden in the lightly shadowed pristine fluffs overhead. Though the day was bright, even the sun seemed particularly friendly as its benevolent warmth and light surrounded us without any apparent glare.

An hour before, I hadn't realized that the day was so particularly peaceful and extraordinarily beautiful. Earlier, I'd heard the sounds of the honking horns and screeching tires.

Now I heard the tones of animated chatter and the laughter of people chorusing above them. I took a deep breath, feeling almost grateful for this opportunity to slow down.

I looked at the little man. He now clutched my arm with the same sense of assurance as my daughter had when she was a one-year-old. Even so, when I carried her five-plus feet off the ground, she was confident that I was in charge of her safety. It was now that I noticed he smelled like my grandfather: talcum powder and Mennen aftershave lotion, an aroma I had missed until just this instant. I wondered how many grandchildren and great-grandchildren he had, and if, like my grandfather, he bounced these children on his lap, told them jokes and played hide-and-seek. If grandchildren were wondering about Grandpa's whereabouts, were others also—his sons and daughters, brothers and sisters, a wife? His gentle yet dignified demeanor touched my heart, and I gently placed my arm in his, offering support as together we focused on the task of placing one foot in front of the other. His body trembled as we crept along, step by step.

The angelic look on the little man's face reminded me of the words of my daughter, as well as other words from a close friend whose card to me had read, "Some of God's angels come to us disguised." I wondered if on this day one had appeared in the form of a little old man wearing a gray wool vest with knobby leather-covered buttons, brown corduroy pants and a brown tweed jacket. Because I was trekking through life with a cellular phone in one hand and tickets for the Concorde in the other it took a helpless, scared and lost person to teach me the real value of time.

The card from my friend had also read, "Leave space in your day for angels to play." I considered the possibility that an angel disguised as a small doddering old man had intervened, just as I had asked, to help me gain perspective. Maybe space is simply time—time to appreciate life, time to live in the moment, time to put someone else's needs ahead of our own. Then the final words from the card, "We are all angels in training." For a moment I considered that perhaps this little man was practicing on me. Quickly I discounted it. It would take an angelic force to supersede my agenda.

Some time later on our journey, just when I began to really enjoy this afternoon "stroll," I heard a woman's frantic and urgent voice in the distance. "Henry, Hennnry, Hennrrrry!" she cried out. Instinct told me this was the voice of alarm. Listening intently to decipher the direction of the voice, I realized it was directly in front of us. The voice grew nearer and nearer, until finally a sweet-looking, little lady, catching sight of my walking partner, ran toward us as frantically as a frail old lady can run. A few wisps of gray hair had escaped her neatly styled bun and her green eyes sparkled with tears of relief. Winded, her cheeks rosy from sprinting, she huffed, "Oh, thank God, praise the Lord!" She momentarily clenched her hands over her chest. "I asked God to send my husband someone to watch over him and my prayer was answered!" She hugged the man; and although I saw no flicker of joyful recognition when she approached, he returned her embrace in befuddled acceptance.

"My husband wandered away from home this morning," she went on breathlessly. "Oh, how rude of me, my name is Nancy. Nancy Marshall." She reached both her hands out to embrace mine. Looking lovingly at the man, she added, "And this is my dear husband . . . "

"Henry," I said, finishing her sentence.

"Yes," she laughed, realizing she had been shouting his name throughout the community just moments ago. "And you are?"

"Bettie," I answered. Before I could say anything further, she explained, "Henry and I had finished breakfast when he said he wanted to take a nap. I went to work in the garden. I wasn't there all that long. When I came in, I just assumed my sweetheart was still napping. It must have been an hour or so before I checked in on him, so I really don't have any idea how long he's been missing, but I've been searching for the last two hours. Oh, you can't believe how frightened I was! Thank you so much!"

"You're very welcome," I replied, feeling just a fraction of her relief myself. "Besides, I'm quite convinced you found us, since, to tell you the truth, I didn't know where I would end up." I glanced around at the scenery one more time, almost disappointed that my serene trip was about to end. "It was quite enjoyable, really. Your Henry gave me a nature tour. He showed me the lovely sights on the campus, a trip for which I am most grateful."

"Yes," she agreed, "my Henry is prone to wandering. Getting lost is his specialty these days; he gets disoriented very easily." As she spoke, she fondly caressed his cheek, held his face momentarily, then glanced from his eyes to mine. "He was a professor at the university over 30 years ago," she said, surveying the beautiful campus around us.

"We've lived in the vicinity ever since that time. It seems he must be reminiscing. Though I can't make out what he says, every time we pass by the campus he starts chattering. Nonstop, I tell you," she said lovingly. She rubbed her husband's hands between hers, searching his distant eyes. "You're remembering something about this place, aren't you honey?" she said respectfully. She neatly tied his scarf about his neck, adjusting it precisely. She looked at me and then at her Henry before she sighed gratefully, "It's all right now, isn't it Henry?" She smiled into Henry's eyes. Though his features didn't otherwise respond, I believe I saw an answer twinkle from their mysterious depths.

She turned to me again and said, "Thank God someone kind enough to help him came along." Her eyes misted again as she looked into mine. "Again, thank you so much."

"You're so very welcome," I reassured her. I looked at my watch; nearly two hours had passed! I watched the two of them, arm-in-arm, toddle down the sidewalk. Even together, they looked like they needed assistance. "Let me help you," I offered. With her husband in between, we made our way to their nearby home. Once there, I helped her settle him comfortably on their front-room sofa. I was moved by the love and warmth between them as they clucked about whether or not Henry wanted to remove his sweater or his neck scarf, which he definitely didn't want to take off. I felt honored that they trusted me to come into their home and invited me to return for a visit in the near future.

On the drive back to my office, my thoughts were filled with the reunited couple. My heart was still warmed by their love and the gift of time each gave to the other. I knew

I wanted to structure my life to have enough time for others, to define the time I share with others as one of the great joys of life.

It was a turning point, one that not only helped me understand a bit more about that angel my daughter said was playing in her heart, but also a bit more about the necessity of taking the *time* to allow angels room to play in our hearts in the first place. Remembering the agitation and frustration of my earlier impatience and frenzy, I realized that I'd been given what I'd asked for—the luxury of not having to worry about the time—if only for a few hours.

I thought about my over-scheduled afternoon, and still I was enveloped in a blanket of peace. The time I took to be kind to the man was not lost. I knew I would have to take stock: Why did I never have enough time? My days were as long as the woman's I'd seen earlier pushing her baby in the stroller. They were as long as the days of the two lovers walking arm-in-arm. They held the same number of hours as those of the businessmen who had been crossing the street; the same as the little old couple. Like everyone else, I had the same 24 hours each day and the same 60 minutes each hour.

I don't really know if the little man was *used* that day to disguise an angel who was teaching me a valuable lesson on the essence of time. I do know that I am thankful for the one that continues to flutter around inside my heart, teaching me to examine my own nature.

10

Money of
My Own

*Love . . . If you don't have it, it doesn't
much matter what else you have.*

—Sir James M. Barrie

"May I help you?" I asked.

It was at one of the *two* jobs I held, but staying in college
was worth it. The first job was cold calling—making calls to
people's homes and asking them if they wanted a subscrip-
tion to one magazine or another. Since the calls were placed
between five and 10 at night, most people considered the
call an intrusion either on their dinner plans, their family

time or both. My job at Wolfe's Department Store was a different matter; it was more like fun than work. My task was to straighten the rows of beautiful garments made from the most refined fabrics and sell them to lovely women with manicured nails and salon-kept hairstyles, women who could afford such things—or who wanted to.

"Oh, I hope so," she said wistfully. She was a pretty woman of about 30. She wore a yellow sundress and white sandals; her long auburn hair hung in soft curls around her shoulders. She pushed a baby stroller that held a bundle of baby covered by a pale blue animal print blanket.

"It's my husband's class reunion in six weeks and I want to look absolutely wonderful for him," she said. "Two months ago I was here and saw a gorgeous peach-colored silk dress. Only after I tried it on did I realize how much it cost, so I was almost relieved when it revealed the extra pounds I was still carrying from my pregnancy. But the dress was so pretty, it motivated me to get back in shape. Now that I am, and with the reunion in just a few weeks, I told myself I better start shopping for a dress to wear. I was hoping that I'd find that dress, though I can't imagine that such an exquisite dress would still be here. But maybe, I thought, just maybe, or you might have something like it."

I admired her overall wholesome appearance, her flawless skin, sparkling eyes, long shining hair, her gentle demeanor and genuine niceness. I also thought going to such lengths to please her husband and to be special for him was a rather romantic gesture. I tried picturing her husband and thought he must be very handsome, well-educated and a loving husband and father. I was sure that he would be the kind of man I would admire.

When the baby stirred, the woman noticed immediately. Leaning over, she stroked the talcum-smelling, picture-perfect baby on his chubby cheek and gently retied the strings to a blue bonnet shielding his eyes from the light. Again the baby stirred, and her hand moved from his cheek to the fine strands of baby-oiled hair that had been brushed to the center of his forehead and formed into a perfect curl. She reached beneath the baby's blanket, retrieved a glass bottle of baby formula, removed the plastic cap, and softly rubbed the baby's lips with the rubber nipple. More interested in sleeping than eating, he turned his little head away from the bottle and resumed a peaceful sleep.

Whispering, she said with a playful sigh, "Wonderful, that means a few more minutes of quiet time!"

Realizing her time without distractions was limited, I said, "Let's look around to see if the dress is still here." We walked through the four rows of racks, but the dress she was looking for was nowhere among the perfectly hung clothes. Her heavy exhale was as lengthy as her deeply drawn inhale. "Oh gosh," she said, obviously disappointed.

"Last week we received a new shipment of silk dresses," I said encouragingly, trying as much to please and appease her as to be helpful. "They're over here, if you'd like to look at them. Maybe we can find something similar, or maybe one you'll like even better." I led her to the rack of new dresses that had just come in. She looked through them slowly, carefully touching the delicate fabrics with her long graceful fingers.

"Oh," she lamented, as she looked over the elegant apparel, "you should have seen *that* dress." Her eyes widened with her smile. She looked around at other things but, still enchanted by the special dress she had seen some weeks back, continued describing it in great detail. Suddenly, it occurred to me that we just might have a couple of these dresses still in the store. Several items had been moved to another department to make room for the new shipment she was now looking through.

"What size do you wear?" I asked.

"Size six," she answered.

"If you don't mind waiting," I said, "I'll have a look in another department. I'll be right back."

When I returned, I found her sitting in a chair patiently waiting for me. It was clear that the peach-colored silk dress with the cloth-covered buttons was the dress of her choice, and she would wait. When she saw me coming with the very dress she had described, she stood up and, with a look of amazement on her face, covered her mouth with both hands.

"Oh," she said excitedly. "That's it! That's the dress!"

"Size six!" I said, gleefully holding it out to her. "And it's on sale, 40 percent off!"

The woman could hardly believe her good fortune. She took the dress and quickly disappeared into the dressing room. Moments later, she emerged to check herself in the full-length mirror. Slowly she turned to observe herself from every angle, carefully scrutinizing the image in the mirror before her. She was right, the dress was absolutely beautiful, and she looked resplendent in it. But it was more than the transformation of the dress from the frame of the hanger to the frame of her body. She felt lovely and elegant in the dress and her face radiated her joy. She looked at me and smiled. No words needed to be exchanged. It was obvious the designer had a woman such as her in mind when fashioning the dress.

"Thank you, thank you so much . . . ," she squinted to read the print on my gold name tag, "Bettie. My name's Molly."

Molly paid in cash, carefully unwrapping a bundle of mostly small bills. She counted out the exact amount needed for the purchase, laying the money on the counter. I wrapped up her beautiful new dress in the lavender-colored, skin-thin, soft tissue paper used by our department and put it in one of the elegantly decorative shopping bags used by our store. As I handed it to her, Molly reached out her hand to touch mine and in a soft, sincere voice she said, "Thank you so much again for all of your help, Bettie. I'm so happy you found this dress for me. I can't wait to wear it."

I was sure that when I was married, like Molly, I would delight in doing special things for my husband. It also dawned on me that helping others feel happy was a better way to earn a living than interrupting someone's dinner plans and family time with magazine sales.

The idea was short-lived.

One evening a few days later, a very handsome man came up to my counter. He tossed a Wolfe's shopping bag on the desk and barked, "This is a return." Through pursed lips, he added, "For cash."

I opened the bag and took out a silk, size-six peach-colored dress. I flipped the tag over, and there, in my hand-writing, were the store code numbers, the date of the sale and my register code.

"All the tags are still on it," a woman's voice said softly. I looked up and saw Molly standing several feet behind him, looking meek and embarrassed. I didn't understand.

"Oh," I said, surprised that the dress was being returned. "Is there something wrong with this dress? If so, we have an alterations department that can fix it for you."

"No, there's nothing wrong with the dress," the man shot back. "No one in her right mind would pay this much for a dress." He went on to say other things, too, all designed for intimidation.

I made the exchange: her dress for her carefully saved money. The man took "his" money, shoved it into his pocket and ordered, "C'mon, let's get out of here." He led the way as they left.

The incident seemed like a scene in a movie that's out of sequence. It was like a Christmas tree with a star but no lights or ornaments. It just didn't fit. In the short time I'd helped Molly, I'd seen only her beauty, her gentle nature and her desire to please her husband. Knowing little else, I assumed the recipient of such love would behave in a way that merited such treatment, that he would treat her in a like manner.

That incident haunted me for several days. It seemed so abrupt, so unjust. My first thoughts centered around how I would feel if this had happened to me. Then I thought about what I could do to avoid such a situation. I concluded that I would not only earn my own money in life, but make my own decisions as well.

Still unable to put the incident out of my mind, I wondered if Molly's husband knew how much thought had gone into her purchase. *If only* he knew the loving actions that went with her purchase, perhaps then he might have let her keep the dress. Maybe he would have handled the situation differently—or at least treated his wife differently. Then again, perhaps he wouldn't have.

Over the following weeks, I saw that the dress was marked down even further. Each time my eyes caught sight of it, I felt a sense of disquiet.

While alphabetizing the returned merchandise slips from our department several days later, I came upon the couple's return receipt. As though it were an omen of some kind, the man's telephone number stood out. Deciding it was a small risk, I called the man at work.

"Sir," I said, "I hope I'm not disturbing you. I'm the salesclerk who waited on you and your wife when you came in to return a dress she purchased."

"Yes, I remember you," came the disgruntled reply. "What do you need?"

"I may be out of line here," I began, "but, well, your wife made such an impression on me, and I thought you ought to know . . ." The line remained silent, so I continued, "What a truly beautiful woman she is, and not only in her outward appearance, but also in the love and devotion she shows to you and your new son. I could tell you weren't happy about the money she had spent on that dress, but it seemed so important to your wife to look beautiful for you at your reunion. She was so pleased to find the price had been substantially discounted." Drawing a deep breath, I continued, "She honestly bought it with you in mind, and now the dress has just been marked down even further." It seemed so logical and simple to me. "Can't you let her have it?" I pleaded. In a last effort to convey my message, I added, "I guess what I'm trying to say is something my father taught me. He said, 'It's good to value the things money can buy, but it's good, too, to check up once in a while and make sure you haven't lost the precious things in life that money can't buy.'"

My hopes rose at what I took as a thoughtful silence. They were crushed when he answered, "You're right, you're out of line. And I think I made my intentions clear when I was in the store. But thanks for thinking of us." With that, he hung up. No "good-bye," just the harsh click of the phone.

His dismissal left me feeling discounted, like an uneducated schoolgirl working in a clothing store. These momentary feelings of low self-esteem were quickly replaced. I knew the risk of calling and wanted him to know what I thought. He was the one who was emotionally illiterate here, not me. It was worth the call, even though I wished things could have turned out differently.

When I came to work a couple of days later, I was greeted by a bouquet of white daisies with a note that read, "Thank you for your thoughtfulness." The card held no signature.

"When did these arrive?" I asked Helen, my coworker.

"Yesterday," she responded with a twinkle in her eyes.

"Do you have any idea who they're from?" I asked.

"We assumed you had a secret admirer!" she replied.

Puzzled, I went about my work as usual.

I was rehanging some apparel when an excited, vaguely familiar voice said, "I was hoping I'd find you here!"

"Oh, it's good to see you again, Molly," I said, surprised. Why hadn't I put it together? The daisies had been from her, a peace offering for her husband's rudeness.

"He bought *it* for me!" she said gleefully. She didn't have any doubts that I'd remember what "it" was as her words burst forth in obvious delight.

Pleasantly stunned, I found myself grinning as widely as Molly. "Oh, I'm so happy for you. That dress was made for you!"

"But that's not all," she went on, unfastening her purse to retrieve something even as she spoke. "In fact, it's not even the best part. I just had to show you. Look at the note he put in with it when he gave it to me." Unconsciously she touched it to her heart, showing how precious it was to her, then thrust it toward me, obviously eager to share her joy.

Still smiling at her happiness, I unfolded it carefully and read the note's bold handwriting.

Darling,

I'm sorry that I've let the pressure of my work and being a good provider cause me to lose sight of just what it is I'm working for. I'm also sorry it took me this long to realize how much you deserve this dress. It's taken me too long to realize a lot of things—including how beautiful you'll look wearing it. Most important, I've realized just how lucky I am to have you and your love. Thank you for loving me as you do.

Yours Forever,

. . . XOXOXO

She watched me as I read it silently, her eyes moist with tears. She was no doubt rereading it with her heart, each word memorized and forever etched there. The fullness of Molly's heart touched me as much as the humility and love of her husband's note.

"Oh Molly," I said, "I'm so happy for you."

"Me, too," she replied. "I just had to let you know. Hey, lovely flowers," she said gazing at the daisies sitting next to the cash register. "Are they from your boyfriend?" Without waiting for a reply, she continued, "You know, my husband sent me a bouquet of roses yesterday. Oh, I just love that man."

I said nothing. It seemed wise not to tell her about the call I made to her husband. Or the white daisies that were from him, a thank you for reminding him how special he was to her.

11

The Blue Ribbon

A moment's insight is sometimes
worth a life's experience.

—Oliver Wendell Holmes

Autumn days are always perfect, and this one was no different. The lazy sun still warmed the skin; the breeze swirling at will through manes of hair was not yet an angry one. Clumps of bigger than life-size leaves—yellow, gold and sienna brown—chased by the unpredictable tantrums of gusty fall winds, tumbled aimlessly down the narrow streets of this seemingly sleepy little village. It was a day that suited this Eastern town where old and majestic trees, now splendidly painted in the vivid colors of fall, shielded from immediate view neatly kept houses with manicured lawns. It all seemed so picture perfect.

"We have wonderful kids and wonderful teachers, and wonderful parents, too," he said. "I know you'll enjoy your time with us." The fatherly superintendent of schools chatted amiably (and nonstop) all the way from the airport to the school where I would conduct a workshop for high school seniors. Was it possible this little pocket of paradise had managed to preserve a sense of innocence for the town, its families and its children? Had this kind and benevolent school leader managed to protect these children from the perils of a global economy, shifting mores and changing family values—and from themselves?

The first thing I noticed as we drove onto the school grounds was the billboard. Just yesterday it had announced the school's next football rival. Now it read, "Welcome, Dr. Youngs."

"Nice touch," I said sincerely. "Thank you."

"Don't thank me," said the superintendent. "Thank Robby Ballen, the student council president."

"Please introduce me if you can," I said.

"Oh, Robby will be around all right. He's everywhere. Quite a leader, that boy. He's been elected student council president three years in a row. That's pretty unusual. In all the years I've been involved in school leadership, I've seen it happen only a couple times. It's a pretty strong vote of confidence from your peers."

"I'll say," I agreed.

We approached the school building, and the superintendent rushed a few steps ahead to open the door for me. The instant I stepped inside a band began playing! I looked up and there, dressed in their school's band uniforms, was a small group of students assembled on my behalf. Delighted, I paused to play center stage to their tribute.

"Wow!" I exclaimed to the smiling and blushing students. "I'm impressed! Thank you for a wonderful welcome." It was then that I noticed the banner above their heads. In addition to a very interesting caricature of me, every student in the school had personally written a short quip to welcome me and signed their name, age and the date.

I turned to the superintendent who simply smiled and shrugged his shoulders. We walked to the auditorium where I would conduct the program for the seniors. We continued down the hall, turned left, went down the next hall, turned right, walked down the next corridor past the cafeteria, then entered the next to the last door on the right. The banner followed the entire way!

"That's a lot of work!" I exclaimed. A lot of paper, too, I thought. "Don't tell me," I said. "This was inspired by Rob, right?"

"Actually, it was," the superintendent replied. "All the students participated in carrying it out obviously, but it was Rob's idea, and it was accomplished through his leadership."

I was testing the microphone and setting up when a voice nearby asked, "Do you need anything? Is there anything I can do to help?"

I fully expected to see a custodian, vice-principal, counselor or any other adult who might have been assigned to oversee my needs for the program. Instead, there stood a handsome, muscular and well-dressed young man. "Hi!" he said, "I'm Rob Ballen."

"Nice to meet you, Rob," I said. "I've heard many good things about you. I'm Bettie Youngs, and yes, there is a way for you to help. A good friend of mine, Helice Bridges, has developed a little exercise that's sort of like an award ceremony. A blue ribbon with the words Who You Are Makes A Difference is used to acknowledge a person for something they've said or done that has made a difference to you. In my workshop with your class today I'll be calling on a number of students, but I need a *volunteer* to start it off. Would you mind if I called on you to come forward first?"

"Oh, that'd be fun!" he said without hesitating or asking anything more about exactly what it was he would be expected to do.

"Good," I said. "I'll count on you then!"

The seniors filed into the auditorium in various states of anticipation and expectation. "Sometimes we don't express what's really in our hearts," I began. "This is particularly true when it comes to telling others, 'Thanks for being there for me, for making a difference in my life.' It's important that we do this. First, it lets a person know that what he did was significant to you. Second, it gives the person the courage and motivation to do it again, to you and to others along the way. We needn't wait for some major event to happen. We can acknowledge others for their acts of kindness, for acting out of integrity—especially when it's not always popular to do so—and when someone accomplishes a worthwhile goal. I'd like to show you a simple exercise that can help you acknowledge someone for making a difference to you in some way. I'd like to ask you to pay close attention to your feelings as we go through this process. I need a volunteer from the audience. Who would like to . . ." Rob's arm shot in the air. ". . . volunteer? Okay, Rob, would you come up, please?" His classmates hooted and cheered and whistled good-naturedly. It was easy to tell that he was well-liked.

Rob came up and stood beside me. The top of my head just barely reached his shoulders. His presence with me and in front of them caused his classmates to giggle nervously and fidget with their belongings. After all, here was their handsome classmate standing beside a visitor who held in her hand a microphone, and who had the ability to call on them in front of their peers. It was their school, however, and they held the power to pay attention in a noisy manner or pay attention in a respectful manner. Power danced between them and me in perfect balance.

"Rob," I said, "I would like you to know that the wonderful welcome that your classmates gave me when I arrived at school today made me feel warmed, honored and welcomed. Since you were the one responsible for organizing it, I would like to thank you for being so thoughtful." My words were met with claps, whistles and cheers. Even so, I knew they were happy it was Robby up there and not them. Now only quiet chatter could be heard among a few friends. "As you can see, I'm holding a blue ribbon with the words, **Who You Are Makes A Difference.** Your leadership actions made a difference to me. Thank you. Because you have acknowledged me, in a sense you have asked that I acknowledge you. Best of all, your actions caused me to want to connect with you and your classmates in a meaningful way. May I pin this ribbon on your shirt?" Little gasps, nervous giggles—and a few good-natured and mild-mannered catcalls—arose from the audience of adolescents.

Rob looked first to me and then glanced over the faces in the audience. "Yeah, sure," he acquiesced. Smiling from ear to ear, he leaned down so I could reach the pocket of his shirt and pin the ribbon on it. All eyes were now upon Robby, all motions stilled by their nervousness. This was far too close for comfort in the minds of these young people still learning the social rules of human touch. Classmates poked each other to distract themselves from getting too close to the experience, no doubt relieved this was happening to Rob and not to them.

I continued the ceremony. "When you take this shirt off, Robby," I said amplifying my voice a bit because of the hoots and howls these "risqué" words brought, "I would like you to remove the ribbon and place it on the mirror in your bathroom so that as you get ready for school each morning, you will be reminded that your thoughtfulness was genuinely appreciated. Your caring actions were important to me."

I backed up a few steps. Now acting from the emotional energy of a speaker, rather than from the personal one-on-one I had just used, I looked at Robby and asked, "How does it feel to be acknowledged in this way?"

"Oh," he said sincerely. "It feels good. I'm not sure if anyone has ever told me 'thank you,' for anything." He became solemn and reflective. Shaking his head, he quietly repeated, "I don't think anyone has told me 'thank you.'" It didn't seem appropriate for me to examine that further, although I'm sure the audience "got it." Here was a young man who had on occasion done many considerate things for others. Yet, Robby hadn't been told—or he didn't hear—their thanks.

"Rob," I continued, "now that we can all see how this exercise works, I'd like for you to call someone up from the audience and acknowledge that person for making a difference to you."

"Oh," said Rob, macho posturing to impress, "that'll be easy. Chad, get your booty up here." Chad, his best friend, bounded up. Once again the classmates cheered and clapped. The two guys playfully punched each other a time or two, then stood at attention in front of me. Standing next to Rob to oversee and assist him with the ceremony, I nodded for him to begin.

"Hey, bud!" Rob began in a voice filled with spunk and spirit, "I've got a blue ribbon here, as you can see, with the words **Who You Are Makes A Difference**." He turned to me and mouthed the words, "Now what do I say?"

"I would like to tell you how you made a difference to me," I instructed.

"Yeah, I'd like to tell you how important you are to me," he mimicked and then added, "And why."

I observed, but said nothing.

"Why you're important to me," he began, looking first at Chad, then the floor, then at the ceiling, then at me, "is because . . ." He stopped, cleared his throat, and tried again. "Why you're important to me is because," and once again he looked first at Chad, then the floor, then at the ceiling, then towards the back of the room and back again at me, "is because . . ." He stopped, cleared his throat, sniffled, and this time Mr. Football used the hand of his "golden arm" to clear away the cloud of tears blurring his vision. The audience watched in disbelief, and perhaps in fear. *Oh, no. Was it possible that their hero, the pillar, was going to cry?*

"Oh Chad, ol' bud," Rob began again, "I've never told you, I never really wanted you to know . . . but you . . . you . . . saved my life. I don't know if you ever knew it, and if you did, you didn't let on. Remember the time last year when I came to your house at 11:30 at night and you knew I had been drinking? You took my car keys from me and though we argued over it, you refused to give them to me. You knew that I couldn't drive and you called my mother, told her that I had fallen asleep and asked if I could spend the night at your house. I never told you, but my parents had gotten in a huge fight that night and my dad said he was leaving. He had filed for divorce. I was so mad and hurt, and I thought, *What will my friends at school think? How can I tell them that my parents are divorcing when my mother is the PTA president and my dad always helps drive us to the football games? Now he's leaving my mother and moving away. My class isn't going to want me to be class president anymore, and . . .*" Rob covered his face with one hand, then letting out a big sigh, continued. "You saved my life, Chad." The silence of the audience blared louder than any words could. Robby, now looking into the eyes of a very shocked Chad continued, "I was going to drive off of old Highway

164 that night. You saved my life." Chad reached over and pulled him into his arms. The two boys hugged each other for what seemed like a very long time.

The audience sat stunned, aghast that their hero had once entertained such thoughts—or was even capable of them.

Now just another teenager, Robby, with shoulders slumped, took a seat.

Chad, still dealing with all this, stood motionless beside me.

"Chad," I said softly. "Here's a blue ribbon for you. I'd like you to acknowledge someone who has made a difference in your life."

It was a fairly sedate Chad that called upon Mr. Hudson.

"I'd like to call up the shop teacher," he said. A bewildered-looking teacher in the second row of the bleachers got up and came forward, taking his place beside Chad.

"Ah, you know that I gave you a hard time all last semester in shop class," Chad stammered. All the students in the audience were all but holding their breath. Though I didn't know the situation at the time, they knew just *who* the shop teacher *was*. "I guess I better begin by saying, I'm sorry," Chad said. "It's just that . . ." he stopped, as though choosing his words carefully.

It caught me by surprise, too, when Chad continued with the words, "*Dad*, it just seemed to me that you'd touch the other guys on the arms or shoulders, or help them with their projects, but you didn't do that for me. It made me so jealous. You stopped touching me when I was in the seventh grade. I thought, *Why do these kids deserve his touch and I don't?* Anyway, I gave you a rough time and I'm sorry. I admire you because you are such a good teacher and all the kids like you and think you're great. I do, too, Dad. I want to give you this blue ribbon because I think you're the best teacher ever. And you're a great dad, too. And I love you. Can I pin this on you?"

It was a meek and tearful father who received the blue ribbon.

"It's your turn, Mr. Hudson," I said.

"I'll call Suzee Merril," said the best teacher at the school.

"Suzee," he said, "as you can see, I'm holding a blue ribbon with the words Who You Are Makes A Difference. I would like to tell you how you made a difference to me. You were the first girl to take shop class, and that was a courageous thing to do. I'd like to . . . "

Suzee called up Bob, her brother. And her brother called up Tammy.

"Tammy," Bob said, "as you can see, I'm holding a blue ribbon with the words Who You Are Makes A Difference. I would like to tell you how you made a difference to me. I'm no Einstein, but here I am, finally a senior, and it's because of you. For the last three years, I got up and came to school only because I knew you'd be here. Though we've broken up and aren't dating anymore," he paused to look to Rebecca, his new girlfriend, sitting nearby with his class ring around her neck and his coat draped around her shoulders, "I know that I'd have dropped out of school, maybe worse, if it hadn't been for you . . ." Though he noticed, he seemed unfazed by his new girlfriend's scowl and look of absolute dejection. He looked again at Tammy and repeated, "If it hadn't been for you."

Tammy stood next to him, her arms tightly hugging her chest. This was difficult enough, loving him still; yet watching as he now dated another classmate was even more painful. Tammy didn't want anyone else. She had hoped to marry her Bob. She was so hurt that she couldn't lift her eyes to his, not even after his kind words. When he said, "You were the most important thing that ever happened to me," her arms unwrapped and followed her hands to her face, where the heavy black mascara and eyeliner she wore was now streaming down. She buried her face in her hands and sobbed uncontrollably. The only boy she had ever loved had confessed her importance—humbly and genuinely. It left her visibly shaken emotionally, but more, her entire body was literally shaking. He pinned the blue ribbon on her collar, looked at her tenderly and said through his own tear-filled eyes, "Thank you for being there for me. I will always love you."

Seventy-one students, hearts now standing at attention, sat bewildered. They were overwhelmed. They knew their own lives were complex, but was it possible that their peers could live in the same sort of inner disarray? And how was it possible that a young person, each and every one of them, could be so special and so meaningful to others?

It was a good place to stop the blue ribbon ceremony and begin my teaching, though much of what they needed to learn had already been accomplished.

As the superintendent drove me to the airport that next day, he said, "I don't know where to begin. Quite honestly, yesterday afternoon opened my eyes. These kids are dealing with a lot more than they let on. I had no idea that under their 'all-is-well' facades, even the brightest students harbor such intense feelings and face such difficult challenges. There's no way I can change all that. I had no idea the depth of the pain so many of these young people harbored. There's no way I can change the nature of their lives. It dawned on me that I'm not making the difference I thought I was. In fact, I no longer believe that I *can* make a difference."

"Sure you can," I said.

"How do you mean?" he asked, looking a bit forlorn.

"A man jogging on the beach one day came across a young boy picking up starfish, frantically slinging them into the ocean," I began, relaying the story, told time and time again. "'I'm afraid your efforts are in vain, young man!' the jogger said as he approached the boy. 'Hundreds of starfish have been washed ashore here, and they're withering fast in the hot sun. Your well-intentioned efforts simply aren't going to make a difference. You might as well run along and play.' The boy surveyed the many starfish stranded on the beach, then looked at the beautiful starfish he was holding. Flinging it into the ocean, he replied optimistically, 'I made a difference to that one!'"

"Unlike the man on the beach who knows all the starfish aren't going to get rescued," countered the superintendent, "and therefore doesn't think it's worth the effort, I *want* to rescue them all. I want my students, all of them, to be healthy, successful and, most of all, happy."

"Oh, Mr. Thomasson," I said. "It's not up to you to rescue. Your job is to teach and prepare these kids to rescue themselves. Just as the boy's singular actions made a difference to each one he touched, each student you touch and better prepare for life's challenges brings you one step closer to achieving your own goal of truly helping them all."

"But just *how* do I prepare them?" he asked sincerely.

"You begin by teaching through your own example," I said to this loving caretaker, thinking how lucky this town was to have him as father-leader to its children. "Don't think the way you maintain the safety of the school—its emotional climate, the attitudes and dedication of your wonderful parents and teachers—goes unnoticed. You are providing a model, a blueprint of a successful community and the elements required to make that community work for every student that attends. The focus on principle-centered values demonstrated daily through your actions and the actions of your staff are often the critical determinants as to whether or not these children will 'wither' or 'swim to safety.' I believe that these students are fortunate to have you. I *know* that you make a difference in their lives daily."

He looked at me in a melancholy way and smiled. "I appreciate what you're saying. Seventy-one hearts were opened yesterday, including mine. Now I see my students and my job in a whole new light." More to himself than to me, he added, "It's time to look a little deeper to see past the surface appearance of these children and offer the additional support and leadership that truly will prepare them for the future in careers *and* in their personal lives."

"It's gratifying to come across leaders such as you who offer hope to all of us with your unwavering commitment to our youth" I told him. "I wish there were more leaders of youth with this type of working devotion. It's people like you who cause me to believe in people and who make what I do worthwhile to me."

We arrived at the airport. In parting, I reached out my hand to shake his hand. It was two large fatherly arms that returned my farewell.

This is *why* I do what I do for a living, I thought. In uncovering the Mr. Thomassons of the world, my heart renews itself. How relevant the line from Richard Dreyfuss in the movie *Mr. Holland's Opus*, "Of all the changes I have helped bring about in others, the greatest change is what has happened within me."

Of What *Use* Is a Cat?

Love doesn't make the world go round.
Love is what makes the ride worthwhile.

—Franklin Jones

"Come, look!" she said, grabbing me by the hand and practically pulling me into her messy room. Quietly and ever so cautiously, she slid open the mirrored door to her closet. Unable to contain her excitement, my daughter shouted victoriously, *"Voilà!"* My eyes followed her long graceful arm to the floor of her closet where a mile-high, mega-ton pile of laundry spilled out of the laundry basket.

"Laundry!" I remarked, wondering what it was she thought my reaction would be to an image I had observed countless times in her closets over the last 20 years. "Oh, Mom," she said, laughing, "You're hopeless! Look again!" Her beautiful blue-green eyes sparkled and a quirky smile made its way across her sensuous, full lips. Her dancing feet sashayed a two-step in anticipation of my seeing whatever it was I was supposed to see. Confounded, I took a step closer and peered in again. Sure enough, there was something other than a pile of laundry-in-waiting. Timbre, her plain gray feline, lay in the middle of the pile. Around her—and on her and over her, with a couple of them nursing—were six newborn kittens. One little fur-ball, blindly in search of milk, helplessly began a feel-as-you-go crawl over the entire length of his mother. Wobbling his way to the top of her head, he promptly hobbled to the edge and fell off. The mother cat winced as two sets of little dagger-like claws dug into her head. She didn't seem to be surprised by the kitten tumbling to the floor. Nor did it bother her.

"Guess that saves you from having to push the little monster off yourself, huh, Timbre?" I remarked, quite sure the kitten's fall was more of a relief than a concern to its mother.

Laughing, Jen poked me in fun and said, "Mom, that's not a very nice thing to say!"

"Honey," I said, "it's the mother-infant relationship that spurred the term unconditional love. At no other time in life do we mothers willingly take so much abuse and lovingly tolerate it!"

"But aren't they just adorable?" my daughter cooed. She was now down on her knees, acting like a doting grandmother to the mother cat whose independence had just been canceled.

"Yes, honey, they are adorable," I agreed.

"Good," she replied. "We're making progress, then. So, which two shall I save for you?"

"Whoa, hold on, sweetie," I said. "Identifying kittens as adorable does not mean I've signed adoption papers."

Using an imagery technique I taught her in childhood, she said to me, "Close your eyes and just picture two darling little kitties sleeping at your toes while you're on the computer, Mom. See them just lying there, keeping your toes warm. Note the peaceful smile on your face! Now you can open your eyes. There, wasn't the thought a pleasant one, Mom?"

I searched for a tactful way of saying no, but settled on, "Jennie, when I closed my eyes just then, two visions came into my mind's eye. First, I saw two cats stranded up a tree, and I didn't have a ladder tall enough to rescue them. I was standing there in a silk dress and high heels, running late for a luncheon with a very handsome man. This was followed by a vision of my frantically searching the neighborhood for two cats who refused to come home until after the last flight to a major international conference I am keynoting has left. There is a look of sheer panic on my face as the minutes tick away and the chances of catching that flight appear bleak to dim. Two docile cats at my feet content in their role of a foot warmer was somehow an image that my mind failed to conjure up. Besides, honey,"

I said, not wanting to discourage an application of a skill I was happy to see her use, "my pets of choice have always been dogs. You know that. You're the one who likes kitties as we can see from what's going on here."

"Oh, Mom. *Please.* Just look at them," she coaxed, reaching down for the tiniest fluffball, a gray kitten with markings identical to its mother. Three of the other kittens were black with a white foot (just as their father had been), one was bright orange, and the other a mixture of orange and white spots. "This little baby was born last. Mommy-cat saved the best for last, didn't you, honey," she said in a voice that she owned when she was just a little girl of six. She kissed the baby cat's face—his head was no bigger than a quarter. Meanwhile, the mother cat kept a watchful eye on her baby, now dangling in mid-air above my daughter's face.

"Looks like she's the runt of the litter, honey," I said, taking note of how carefully and lovingly my daughter handled the tiny creature. I could tell that this particular kitten held a special place in her heart. Perhaps this affection was because it was a miniature version of its mother, a spitting image, hair for hair.

Trying once again, she asked, "Mother, won't you just take two kitties, *only* two? I've searched my heart and I can't bring myself to give away *all* of Timbre's kittens. While I can keep the mother cat and her sister, I just can't ask my roommate to live with *four* cats. I know that I have to find homes for four of them. That will be hard enough, but I want to keep two of my cat's babies so badly. Won't you keep *just* two for me for a while? Will you try it, Mom, *please?* I honestly know what a sacrifice it will be for you, especially since you don't much enjoy cats."

Don't much enjoy cats! What an understatement. Disdain is more like it. I was surrounded by cats while growing up. In our family, all cats stayed outside. *No cats in the house* was the rule, and an okay one by me. Other than keeping the mouse population in check, what good was a cat anyway? As a pet, they *can't* even compare to a dog. A dog can be trained to sit up, lie down, roll over and shake hands—on command. They'll walk to the mailbox and back with you and retrieve the newspaper in the morning. Try asking a cat to do this. Can you take your cat for a run? How about for a walk? To the park? Play fetch-the-stick in the stream? Not even. That's my point. Of what use is a cat for a pet? It's not like they're loyal creatures. How many cats have you seen lying on the front steps, head on their paws, looking forlorn, patiently and diligently waiting for their master to come home—then, once they see their master, jump around in affection, so happy and pleased? Not! Other than following you when you have food in your hands, are they likely to follow you around? No. Feel like cuddling one of these furry little creatures? Look else-where. When a cat decides she wants some affection, she'll look you up, walk back and forth around your legs and rub her shedding hair all over your pant leg. Try to pick up this same cat, and she'll be on a full run in the opposite direction. Cats—bah, humbug. They're too independent for me.

Jennifer studied me closely to see if it was time to pitch her closing line on the deal. Seeing that I wasn't ready to sign on the dotted line, she prompted, "How can I impress upon you how so very important this is for me to keep two of my cat's kittens? Mother, *please* say yes."

"I just can't Jennifer," I said softly. "You know that I travel quite frequently and . . ."

"Precisely!" said the master saleswoman who knew exactly how to play me. "That's the beauty of having cats for pets, Mother. They don't eat much, you can leave ample food and water out when you're gone for a couple of days without worry, and they're very independent. A cat is a perfect pet for you. And with two, they'll keep each other company and never be lonely. It's so ideal!"

Jen was ideal. Perhaps it was her look of sincerity, or those big expressive (and now pleading) eyes, or the angelic voice (now with a twinge of sadness) that softened my heart. Whatever it was, I found myself in an impossible position, but I wanted to resolve it in a favorable way. It was her first time living away from home. I wanted her to be happy and to concentrate on school and her job. I knew it was out of the question that the two baby kittens could be with her. It was cumbersome enough that she kept the two bigger cats in her small bedroom.

"I can't Jen," I said again, bending down to pick up a little orange vertebrate that weighed all of three ounces.

Instantly recovering from her "I'll-be-so-saddened-if-you-don't-take-two-kittens" demeanor, she enthusiastically remarked, "I knew you'd like him!"

What could I do?

"Okay," I said reluctantly, figuring I'd take them back home and give them to friends or anyone who would have them. "I'll take that little orange thing. Should we call it 'Pumpkin' in honor of the kitty you had when you were eight?"

"Oh, yes," my daughter said humbly, putting her arms around me and laying her head gently on my shoulder. "Thank you for remembering my heart, Mom." She looked at me lovingly and said tenderly, "Mom, you're the best."

"And don't you forget it!" I said playfully, returning her hug of affection.

Because I had been referring to each kitten as an "it" she mocked me saying, "*It* is a kitten, Mother. This *it* is now named Pumpkin."

"Yes, *it* is a Pumpkin, now," I confirmed, resigning myself to the notion that these little hairballs were all too quickly moving from animated creatures to *my* animated creatures. I sighed deeply and added, "I guess I'll take the little black *it*—the one with the longest hair. He looks like a little panther. Let's call him Midnight."

Elated, she said, "It's a deal! Mom, I love you. Thank you for doing this."

"It's going to cost you," I teased.

"Put it on my tab," she said. "What was it that *Newsweek* published about the cost of raising a child? They estimated that to be about $312,000. So what's a few hundred dollars more? Besides, look at it this way, Mom," she said turning her head to "look at it" sideways, then laughing at her own humor, "making an investment in me is making an invest-ment in *your* future. Someday it'll pay off. Remember, there'll come a time when I'll have to make a decision as to whether to buy you a cheap ol' wooden cane or a sturdy metal one, maybe even with a felt tip at the end so you don't annoy the passersby—though you probably wouldn't mind if you did!"

"Yes, well, I'd say my giving in to two of your kitties —for God knows how long—has sealed my fate. I want a diamond-studded gold cane with my name engraved on it. No felt tip, please."

"Consider it done, Mom," my daughter said laughing, raising her hand for a high-five.

How I loved this young woman. I was as malleable in her hands now that she was 20 years old, as I was when she was 20 days.

Six weeks later I went back to retrieve the two baby kittens.

I could hardly believe what had transpired and was upset about it, too. Jennifer had given away four of the kitties as planned. Also as planned, she kept Pumpkin, the orange male. But there waiting with him was the ordinary little gray female kitten, now named Otis (another name recycled from another previous pet).

I was not at all pleased. If I were to inherit two cats, neither of whom I really wanted, at least they could be attractive. A plain-Jane cat was going to be difficult to give away.

"What happened to my Midnight?" I asked in my best "pay-attention-because-Mother-is-grumpy" voice.

"Mom, I made a decision in your best interest," my daughter, now in the role of mother, said confidently. "These are the two most loving kittens in the litter. I knew that they may have a hard time getting your love, so they needed to know the *feel* of love and affection—enough to go and get it when *they* needed it. Mom, they are so loving that even if *you* refuse to love these kittens, they'll love *you.*" Upon hearing my daughter's voice, the kittens raced down the hallway. With the speed of a bullet, they bounded up into her lap. Instantly, their motors began whirring. "You see, Mom," she said, fully aware that their actions couldn't have been better timed. Even so, she knew my disappointment. "Trust me," she said softly, soothing the adult-child (me) pouting next to her and, in the process, delicately transferring the two little kittens from her lap into mine. Tears filled her eyes and she added softly, "They'll grow on you."

On the flight back to San Diego, the two wee orphaned kittens—who just this morning had been separated both from their birth mother and earth mother—sat in a cold plastic cage under the passenger's seat in front of me. Frightened, but curious, they peered out at the giant feet— absent of bodies and faces—all around them, mine included. Poor little things, just this morning the kittens had been part of a happy family. Now they were without their family, and their happiness, too. Here they were amidst strangers, abducted by an alien force who didn't find them adorable and didn't even like their species. I felt sorry for them. What an awful life they're going to have, I thought.

I studied the little gray female. Your basic gray cat. "How original. It must be boring to be an ordinary gray cat," I said to Otis, who at the sound of my voice softly whimpered and began crying. I quickly looked at Pumpkin. "You

have possibilities," I told him. "I'm sure *someone* will like
you." If anyone wanted a *male* cat. Oh great, I thought.
He'll roam the neighborhood, randomly coming home
when *he* wants, and when he does, he'll terrorize the beautiful birds I've so carefully managed to attract to my backyard. The female cat will have kittens, and then I'll be stuck
with more cats. I'd have to neuter and spay them as well,
and if I didn't want my furniture ruined, I'd have to have
them declawed, and all those shots, and the kitty litter, and
. . . oh my, what did I get myself into? All the way back to
San Diego, I thought about their adoption—into someone
else's life.

Why had I said yes?

Once home, both kittens scampered away within
moments of my taking them out them out of the cage, dis-
appearing into other rooms of the house. Oh well, I thought,
they'll show up when they're hungry. Storing their travel
cage in my daughter's now nearly empty closet, I discovered them. Both kittens had jumped up on my daughter's
bed and snuggled deeply into the belly of a stuffed animal
—one that approximated both the size and look of their
absent mother. The vision of their outstretched legs
straddling, clutching and clinging to something—anything
furry—brought tears to my eyes. I remembered the loneliness I felt the first night after my daughter moved to attend
school nearly 2,000 miles away from home. Now these two
dependent little creatures were also 2,000 miles away from
home and everything that once comforted them.

My heart went out to them. So much so, that I promptly
went to the store and purchased special food designed for

kittens, a bottle of fortified milk, a soft bed with a fleece lining and an assortment of toys.

That evening, I took their little basket-bed into my bedroom, set it beside my bed and extended my hand across their little bodies for the sake of reassurance. This went on for several nights. Well, actually for a full two weeks, but I mean, they had never been away from their mother before, nor the constant coddling of my daughter. When they wanted to sit on my lap and lay their little heads near my hands as I worked on the computer over the next several days, how could I refuse? They needed comforting. Sometime in the next couple of days when I was not so busy though, I would call around to find a new home for them.

The reason I took so much care to read the labels on the special food I bought for them every time I shopped for groceries was because they weren't eating very well. They were homesick and heart-sore, and they had just been weaned. Since they were little and fragile and needed adequate nourishment to grow healthy and strong, only the best nutrition would do. Even if I were going to give them away, they needed their shots for their next-in-line parents, so how could I not take them to the vet? They were so tender and sore and not feeling all that well from their shots, how could I refuse their wanting to snuggle on my lap as I read that evening? How was I to know that they would want to do this every night? How was I to know that because it felt so good for me, too, that it would become a nightly ritual—one that I would welcome?

My home was a new environment for the kittens, and they moved about with great trepidation. When they heard a frightening sound, they ran for cover. Even a falling leaf from an indoor plant sent them scurrying under the furniture, though they preferred height over taking cover under something near the floor level. How could I not buy that five-foot high cat climber—the one with the sleeping basket on top, a paw scratcher at the base, a peek-a-boo den and a miniature trampoline in the center? Safety and sleeping is important but these were active, growing children. Plus, having fun in their room was one thing, but they liked being where they could see me. When they looked the house over for something portable to play with . . . I needed to buy them some additional toys as well.

Their favorite toy was the tiny mouse, bathed in catnip, attached to the string with the feathers—with me at the other end. So much so, that each day around noontime, they retrieved it from where it was stored, dragged it into my office and sat waiting for me to notice.

And notice I did. They so enjoyed our playing together with this toy . . . almost as much as I did. Around and around and around I turned; in hot pursuit, they mercilessly chased the stuffed mouse, from whose ears sprouted pink and silver feathers. They ran so hard and so fast, crashing into each other and me. Eventually they tumbled over each other in dizziness. Every day we played this game. Twirl around, jump up, chase, bounce, twirl around and around and around . . . play and play . . .

One day we were playing as usual, when I heard in the distance the resplendent and enchanting, blissful laughter of a child—a gloriously guttural sound of joyousness. The purity and innocence of this gleeful laughter from a little girl was simply captivating. It momentarily startled me. I stopped and lay still for a moment, for I was down on the floor with two cats tumbling over me, frantic in their attempt to fetch the toy in my hand. I listened and listened. It was then that I discovered *this rapturous sound . . . was my own!*

So this is their gift to me, I thought. They take from me the love they need—the love they've been conditioned to by my daughter—and they elicit my loving them in return. This exchange proffers me playfulness and joy, something so very precious and dear to me that I won't allow myself to be without it.

It was a revealing moment.

I looked to my two cats, now motionless, watching my every blink. I had been stepmother to these two little creatures for a long time. Acknowledging the joy and fun they brought forth in me, I knew it was a feeling I wanted to experience again and again. This should have been evident: days had turned into weeks, the weeks into four months. Giving them up was no longer an option. And so it was that this day I signed their adoption with my heart and gladly assumed their caretaking.

Antoine de Saint-Exupéry's classic fable, *The Little Prince*, tells of the little prince who wants, for his own, something that is "unique in all the world." He comes upon a beautiful flower unlike any he had ever seen before. He is captivated by this flower. You can only imagine his happiness when she tells him that she is one-of-a-kind. She makes ceaseless demands of him. He is to water her, shield her from the hot sun, pick caterpillars from her—but only those that threaten to eat from her stems; he is not to pick those that eat the insects that eat her leaves. The Little Prince does these things for her and in time comes to love her.

One day he finds an entire field of flowers exactly like his flower. He is disappointed and saddened. While he thought he had a rose that was unique in all the world, she is but a "common rose." He sits down and cries. A wise old fox happens along and upon learning why the Little Prince is sad, proceeds to teach him an insightful lesson, promising to share with him a secret when he has done so. When the fox is satisfied that the Little Prince has learned the lesson he intended, he instructs the Little Prince to go back and again look at the field of roses. The fox counsels him to not look with his eyes, but with his heart. Looking once again at the field of roses, the Little Prince is surprised by what he sees. "You are not at all like my rose," he remarks. "You are beautiful, but you are empty to be sure. An ordinary passerby would think that my rose looked just like you, but in herself alone she is more important than all the hundreds of you because it is she that I have watered . . . because it is she that I have sheltered behind the screen . . . because it is she that I have listened to, when she grumbled, or boasted, or even sometimes when she said nothing. Because she is my rose."

"Here, then, is a very simple secret," says the fox keeping his promise. "It is only with the heart that one can see rightly; what is essential is invisible to the eye."

This French children's classic teaches that it is because the Little Prince tended his rose and cared for her in so many ways that he saw her differently. And so it is with my Otis and Pumpkin.

When my dog died of old age and my daughter left for school, I thought I both needed and wanted a time without pets. When my daughter successfully persuaded me to take two kitties, I thought at first I would feel burdened by their care. To the contrary, I do not find the responsibility for their caretaking burdensome or bothersome. In fact, I have found great joy in it. Added to this is the satisfaction I feel watching their endless play and the delight I feel when I hear them come on a full run down the hallway as I come in.

Like the built-in bookshelves, both of my cats have become a permanent fixture in my office. As I put these very words on paper, Pumpkin—or Big Ol' Fat-Cat as I sometimes call him—is asleep on my desk with his ever-growing head on the rim of the keyboard. He's made it his solemn duty to protect me from the fax machine, the laser printer, the ringing phones and any insect or hummingbird buzzing around the outside of my window. Motions or sounds from any of these noise-makers will bring a furried pounce, his goal being to still them.

Otis, the little gray female kitten, is laying on her favorite soft blanket, catnapping in my top desk drawer, her purring motor fervently humming. When she feels she's gone too long without attention, she edges her head beneath my hand to get her head and body scratched and rubbed.

Ever curious, both cats inspect all deliveries, large and small. It is their duty to greet the mailman, the Federal Express delivery person, the secretary, the accountant and my assistant—all of whom know them by name.

Jennifer was right: The kittens have "grown on me." I am smitten. And yet, when I look at my cats, it is through the eyes of love for my daughter that I see them. This causes me to reflect on my daughter and the brand of love she offers. Just as she willfully loved these kittens into being loving—with my ownership of them in mind—she has willfully expanded my heart's ability to love, too. I am grateful that of all the people who know me and love me, she knows me most and loves me the best. What an extraordinary gift she is to me; I am a far better person than I might have been without her.

It was never her intention to reclaim motherhood of these cats. She simply couldn't give them up and had decided now that she was off to college I might as well parent her "children." Because she *knows* me, she conditioned the cats with my personality in mind. Contrary to that day I brought the cats home with me and thought that they would have an awful life, she *knew* better. They have not had an awful life at all. In fact, what great lives they have.

And, yes, as I write this, just as when she asked me to close my eyes and "picture two darling little kitties asleep . . . just laying there". . . that's exactly what they're doing, right here beside me. And yes, there is a peaceful smile on my face.

And in my heart.

13 Gluteus Maximus

The more of life you master, the less of life you fear.

—Source Unknown

I had just completed my workshop at a regional conference for middle- and upper-management personnel on the topic of "Excellence in Our Professional Lives." The luncheon was about to begin. I quickly found my way to the speaker's table and took my seat. Here now was the noontime keynote, "Excellence in Our Personal Lives."

"You know your way around the boardroom, but do you know your way around your body?" the speaker began.

"Do you have as much influence over your muscles as you do your staff? Do your gluteus maximus and adductor brevis do what you want them to do?" These questions sounded rather interesting, if not erotic. I didn't know the answers but was intrigued enough to find them.

I grew up healthy and strong and had greatly valued my body's contribution of energy, stamina and overall wellness all my life. Early in childhood I was taught to take responsibility for the care of my health and well-being, and I had. But these were questions of a different nature. The speaker challenged us to consider the relationship between the body's optimal physical performance and personal excellence—through disciplining and strengthening our muscles. He had piqued my attention. I didn't know my gluteus from a maximus.

I decided to join a workout center.

The membership included two sessions with a personal trainer.

"The goal of this exercise," the lovely woman with an incredibly toned and fit body said, "is the deltoid, the triangular muscle that defines your shoulder. It's a single muscle, but it has three distinct heads that insert at the same place on your upper arm but originate at different sites: the anterior head originates at the collarbone and helps you raise your arm up and forward or rotate it inward. The posterior head originates on the shoulder blade and pulls your arm back or rotates it outward. The lateral, or middle, head lifts your arm to the side and assists the other two heads."

"Wow," I remarked. "I just want to make sure I don't have flabby arms."

Not amused, she retorted, "Yes, that's the goal, but shoulder work should always be complemented with rotator-cuff training to stabilize the joint and keep it healthy."

"I see," I said, scanning the 40-plus machines in the room, wondering which one was designed to train the rotator cuff.

"A lot of people make the mistake of working only what they see," she continued. "They want instant results."

I was certain I wanted to see instant results. She must have read my thoughts.

"Uneven lifting leads to injuries and muscular imbalance. You end up hunched over," she said, pointing to a man nearby whose biceps were so large they caused his arms to stick out nearly two feet from his body. The back of his neck was so thick that his head appeared permanently tilted in the direction of the floor. Leaning against the wall to keep from falling, he bent over and adjusted his knee brace. Then he stood erect and, with a walk resembling a gorilla's, he and his muscles meandered over to the water fountain.

"Got it," I said, convinced. "Show me what I need to do to maintain *balance.*"

"You have to work all three muscle heads, which creates symmetry, prevents injury and builds functional strength for lifting and carrying."

"That's good," I said flippantly. "My briefcase weighs anywhere from 25 to 40 pounds on any given day! It's very important that I be able to lift it!"

"It's important," she said, once again ignoring my comment, "to prefatigue a muscle by first isolating it and then enlisting assistance from other muscles."

"Prefatigue it?" I queried. "That's easy. By the time I get to the workout center, my entire body is prefatigued!" I looked at the large clock nearby and was dismayed to learn that only nine minutes had passed since I began my session with her.

My energy level must have been noticeably low. She asked, "How did you fuel your body in preparation for your workout this morning?"

"My body wakes up at 6:30 A.M., but my taste buds sleep in until around 10:30," I said. "But you'll be pleased to note that I ate breakfast *this* morning. Bran cereal, no less."

Though I was impressed, she wasn't. "If you want to maximize your workout time," the trainer said, "if you want to get the most work from your muscles, to help them respond to the grueling performance you're asking of them, you must fuel your body *correctly*. Otherwise, working out can cause wear and tear on the body. Your body needs energy."

Jesting, I asked, "I guess if I told you I had a cappuccino to perk me up for this, you wouldn't approve, huh?"

She rolled her eyes and went on. "I suggest six to eight egg whites half an hour before you come to the workout center."

"Egg whites?" I asked. I had once dated a man who cracked six to eight fresh eggs each morning, drained the egg whites into a glass and swallowed them in two gulps. He served the yolks to his cats.

"I'm not sure if I can do that," I said, repulsed. "Surely technology has advanced to the point of putting protein in a capsule."

"Just buy a gallon of pasteurized egg whites," she remarked matter-of-factly. "This way you need only pour yourself an eight-ounce glass prior to working out." I was hoping I hadn't thrown out the pamphlet on *Staying Fit WITHOUT Working Out.*

"I want you to understand how each of your body's muscles function," she said earnestly. "When you know your way around your body and know what it's designed to do, you not only respect it, but you train it accordingly. At that point," she added, "you'll fuel your body efficiently so it can do what you're asking of it."

"Got it," I said, certain that I needed a better motivator than working out to get me to swallow egg whites.

"A rigorous workout three to four times a week is all you really need," she added.

"Are you sure that fitness can't be accomplished through rigorous *play?*" I asked. "You know, tennis, racquetball, sex?"

"Well," she said, finally breaking a smile, "I'm sure that once upon a time mankind's rigorous daily work exercised his body and that was all that was needed. Today we live a more sedentary life, and we need to come to the gym more often." There was nothing sedentary about my life. I *ran* through airports with luggage in one hand and a briefcase in the other. I logged as many miles on the stairways in a week (both in my home and in my office) as gold medalist Dan Jansen did in a week on his skates. My mind drifted momentarily to the return-to-nature vacation I took last year, when I dangled from the edge of a cliff, rafted across great river rapids and hiked through a dense verdant rain

forest. My life was anything but sedentary. My letter to
Santa Claus this year asked for one hour of boredom.

"I'll show you how to use one head of the deltoid to start,
then the others to finish the job," she continued, interrupting
the list I was compiling in my head as to why I might not
return to the workout center. "Because the lateral head is the
hardest to work correctly, I like to target it first while it's
fresh, then move on to the often-overlooked posterior head.
Then we'll polish off the set with an exercise, probably the
standing military press, which works all three heads."

Oh my gosh, I thought. She's been in the army. Just my
luck. She's probably been a drill sergeant.

"Another mistake often made in shoulder training," she
said, failing to take notice of the look of alarm on my face,
"is to lift too much weight."

"Don't worry about me on that one," I said.

Ignoring me, she continued, "It's a small muscle with a
fragile joint. So it's safer and more effective to use a routine
that prefatigues part of the muscle than to lift 'heavy.'"

"I stopped 'lifting heavy' when my toddler learned independence," I said. By now feeling as much emotional
duress as physical duress, I searched the clock for relief. A
total of 17 minutes had passed.

Aside from thinking this session would never end, I was
feeling like a neophyte. I searched for a term I was familiar
with. "What about the biceps?" I asked, certain of where
they were located. I had been doing biceps curls and had it
down pat.

"Yes, the biceps are important," she said, "but they don't
operate alone. Here," she said, pulling my arm out to the

side. "To better understand the design of your arms, relax them at your sides, palms facing inward. Turn your palms so that they face forward. You'll notice that the forearms angle slightly away from the body. This is called the carrying angle, and it's greater in women, who average 15 degrees, than in men, who average 5 degrees. This discrepancy is thought to be related to the greater relative width of a woman's pelvis. Now turn your hands so your palms face backward, and the angle will disappear. Be careful not to turn your shoulders inward. This could exacerbate the common problem of rounded shoulders and a collapsed chest."

Immediately alarmed, I said, "Excuse me? Can you repeat that?" I liked my chest and wasn't about to do something to collapse it. "I want to make absolutely sure I do this exercise correctly," I said, laughing nervously.

"Good," she said. "All three arm muscles involved in the standard biceps curl—the brachialis, biceps brachii and brachioradialis—cross the elbow in the front."

This all sounded like a foreign language to me. I had no idea what she was saying. "I'm afraid my doctorate degree didn't cover the material you're teaching," I said. "Perhaps you'd better think of me as a second-grader in this subject. I get the feeling that I've been doing exercise all wrong and have wasted a lot of time." I felt totally inadequate after she showed me the correct way to do this exercise. "I could just as well have been at the beach," I lamented.

"Yes, but you wouldn't look like you do now," she said. "You're in good shape, all we have to do is improve a couple of things. You're lucky, some people need to work on an entire 'new' self."

I hoped that her expectations for the "new and improved" me didn't include a body like the woman standing next to me—who just last evening had won the Women's Body Building Championships and whose voice was deeper than any guys I knew. I said, "I really do not want to look like that." Just as I was staring at the new female champion's bigger-muscles-through-steroids body, a *very* fit man walked by. I studied him for a moment and said eagerly, "Though I wouldn't mind my butt looking like that!"

"Yes," she said, shaking her head. "Well, then, we'll start with your inner thigh muscle."

"Okay!" I said. I was definitely fired up now.

"The adductors take part in almost every movement of the hip and knee," she said. "Plus, they act as stabilizers. The stronger they are, the more effective all your glute and hamstring training will be. As the gluteus maximus and hamstrings work to lift and lower your hips during exercise, your hip adductors, the adductor brevis, adductor longus, adductor magnus, pectineus and gracilis, work as stabilizers to . . ."

As I left the gym my mind was somewhat confused. I wondered if there might be an alternative, short of memorizing *Gray's Human Anatomy,* that would assist me in becoming an expert on my own body. Beginning to feel muscles I never knew existed, I decided to sort out my deltoids from my trapezoids, my gluteus from my maximus— while treating myself to a massage.

My masseuse met me in the inviting reception area and led me down the plushly carpeted hall into a small comfortable room with smooth white linens covering the massage table in the center. Soft music combined with nature sounds played quietly in the background—a trickle of a babbling brook, birds singing, waves crashing—very different than the sounds of Oingo Boingo playing at the gym.

My masseuse for the hour was an attractive athletic woman in her mid-40s. Her bronze complexion and sun-streaked hair gave away her love for time spent outdoors. She handed me a cotton sheet and showed me where I could hang my clothes and place my gym bag. Anticipating my question of whether to take off everything, she said gently, "This is a nonsexual massage. You can leave your underwear on if you are uncomfortable with your body being naked, although it's easier for me if you don't." She turned and carefully closed the door behind her.

I undressed and climbed up onto the massage table, covered myself with the fluffy white sheet she had given me, and placed my face in a cushioned oval frame that allowed me to lie comfortably face down. I closed my eyes and allowed myself to drift into the soothing music, letting my mind create the beautiful images the sounds inspired. The masseuse knocked lightly on the door and then entered. She asked if there were any specific areas that I would like her to concentrate on. As she covered her hands in warm oil, and then began skillfully stroking the small muscles of my toes and feet, I told her about my desire to know and understand my body on a deeper level and about my experience at the gym. The concept of looking at my body from such a complex perspective was informative, yet it left me feeling more unfamiliar with myself than when I began.

She continued working silently on the muscles in my legs, then said, "Maybe rather than looking at your body in a more complex way, simplifying might be the answer."

"Simplifying? What do you mean?" I asked, interested in her viewpoint.

"Well, what's something you understand very well?"

Almost immediately I answered, "How to run a busy office and a complex business." I could tell by her tone she was on to something.

"What would you define as the nature of a business?" she asked.

"Ideally, it's a group of individuals working together as a unit toward one common goal," I answered.

"Isn't that what your body is also: a group of individual parts, each with specific jobs to do, that allows you to do the everyday things you do and be the person you are?" she asked. "Consider each part of your body: your hands, your feet, fingers, toes, eyes, ears, mouth and nose. Each is like an individual employee with her own skills and her own résumé of accomplishments. The underlying muscles allow each to do their job." I smiled to myself at this notion of writing a résumé for my different body parts. It was an odd analogy, but I saw its value.

Her hands continued working discerningly as she spoke. "Think of each body part and all the things they have done for you throughout your lifetime. What value or price can you put on such service? How much are your arms and hands worth, or your legs, or your eyes? Do you think a person with all the money in the world but without any of these healthy, functional body parts, would gladly exchange all she had for the simple but priceless gifts our body parts give to us daily?" My mind followed her logic and line of reasoning.

As I tried this new perspective on, I felt a sense of great appreciation and respect for my body. It was as if my body was a separate entity, an individual in a partnership with my conscience. Finally, the masseuse said, "I think you understand where I'm going with this. You seem to be a person who is at peace with your body, that's nice. Too often I work with both men and women who, for whatever reason, have nothing but disdain for their bodies. I think the first step to understanding and knowing our bodies is to look at each element with respect. Think of it in terms of your ally and companion, and refuse to have an adversarial relationship with it." With that said, she focused on my massage and left me to contemplate her words with the calming sounds of the soothing music my only distraction.

I thought about it. I love my hands that allow me to put the words of my heart on paper. I love my arms that cradled my newborn babe, that find pleasure in wrapping themselves knowingly around friends and family. I love my eyes for allowing me to see the beautiful sights of this world from sunsets and mountain ranges to the faces of friends, family and others. I love my legs that have run races, walked on the beach and carried me over a million miles in the course of my life.

I liked her idea of seeing our bodies as an ally. Each individual is a composite of soul (consciousness) and body in partnership. This perspective allows us a new relationship with our bodies, starting with appreciation for the specific parts of our body which allow us to accomplish even our everyday physical activities.

This appreciation gave way to a real desire to discipline my various muscles and to keep them fit, healthy, able to perform all that I required of them. It was the reason—the motivation—to go to the gym.

Simplicity sometimes is the key to understanding what often seems complex. I'll continue to learn and explore the complex attributes of my body, but I believe what my masseuse said is true: The first step to understanding and knowing my body is to begin simply with love and respect for the priceless gifts each part gives daily. It is only then that my heart would be up to the task of keeping my body in its highest form and level of fitness and wellness.

The workshop presenter was right: "When you know your way around your body, what it's designed to do, you not only respect it, but you'll train it accordingly." I know that I'll care for the muscles in my body; I have so much yet to do—there are many people to hold, beaches to walk, sunsets to see, mountains to climb.

Pasteurized egg whites aren't really that bad. You just need to gulp them quickly. I'm off to the workout center. Today is the day I work on strengthening my gastrocnemius and soleus. . . .

14

Plan B: Take a Man Along

We don't receive wisdom; we must discover it for ourselves after a journey that no one can take for us or spare us.

—Marcel Proust

"I'm just so infuriated by the whole thing!" Tina said. "He owes me this money. It's wrong of him not to pay me."

"Can he pay you?" I asked. "Does he have the money?"

"Sure he does," she confirmed without a trace of doubt in her voice. "He just won't."

"Why?" I asked. "*Why* is he being so belligerent?"

"It's a matter of integrity," Tina said, "of which he has little. Though I worked for Nick, I was actually hired by his partner, Tim, so Nick feels he doesn't hold the same responsibility to me as does Tim. As you know, Nick bought Tim out of the company. It's quite a bit of money that the partnership owes me. I'm probably also a bit to blame. Because Nick has such a combative style about him, I'm afraid I've been more lenient with him than I should. Because I have, he may feel that I'll eventually tire of chasing him down to collect it. Anyway, my plan has been to simply persist in tracking him down. So far, no luck."

"How can you exert more muscle?" I asked.

"I've considered going to the labor board," she said, "but it takes so long to get paid that way and I really need the money now—though I might have to resort to that. It's really not a very good alternative for me. I'm *so* frustrated by this runaround!" Looking defeated, she asked, "What would you do?"

"Resort to Plan B," I replied.

"What do you mean?" she asked.

"Well, since Plan A has obviously failed, it seems like you'll have to find a better alternative."

"Which is?" she inquired.

"You need to get him to take you seriously," I suggested. "But first, you'll need to get his attention."

"Let me think how I might do this . . ." She chewed her bottom lip, and then said gleefully, "I could bring a bouncer with me."

"Now there's an idea," I said, smiling with shared amusement. We were by now two women engaged in girl talk, brainstorming the resolution of an issue that, unfortunately, we both knew all too well.

"You know, that *would* be effective," Tina persisted.

"I think so," I said half-laughing. I knew it was true. A male presence would make a difference. "Actually, the presence of a man might just be the answer," I said earnestly.

"Bring a man with me . . . that feels so terrible, to be victimized because of your gender," Tina said, feeling diminished. "Has anything like this ever happened to you?"

"Sure," I answered, "but not more than once in the same situation!"

"Really," asked Tina. "Tell me when. What did you do?"

"It's been my experience that the cost of servicing my car is directly related to whether or not I'm alone or with a man at the time I drop it off," I began. "It seems that if I'm alone when I can take my car in for routine service that supposedly has a set price, sometime during the day I'll get a call from a service department with the message that some other repair—generally very expensive and illogical to me—is needed. If I have a male friend stop by to assess what needs to be done, the repair becomes less necessary. I may be told, for example, that I urgently need new brake pads. My male friend is told I could probably get another 10,000 miles or so before they actually need to be replaced. Basically, the number of repairs, parts needed, service time required and the actual cost to me is significantly less if I have a male friend take responsibility for overseeing the servicing of the car."

Not at all surprised, Tina said, "Oh, yeah, that always happens to me. There's no way around it. I can't think of one woman who hasn't had the same experience at a car service shop."

"Well," I retorted, "it made me upset, and I decided *enough!*"

She looked at me. "Tell me you found a way to make it stop without having a man front for you," she teased, but with obvious interest in knowing more.

"I did, but it took several attempts," I said. "Because being a woman meant that the number of items and their cost were almost always more than what I was told at the time I dropped the car off, and because on far too many occasions things that I asked for didn't get done—clocks set, the car washed and so on—I let them know *who* they were dealing with. I went in and said, 'Hi, I'm *Dr. Youngs.* I'm a *professional speaker* and *writer,* and if you don't fix my car right and charge me fairly, I'm going to put a sign on it that says, *I service my car at XXX dealership and they're a rip-off.* When I speak to groups of professionals in this town, I'll tell them about your shoddy practice. Then, I'm going to write an article about *your* dealership and get it published in the *city's* most popular and best read *magazine!'*"

"Wow!" said Tina, nearly rolling on the floor with laughter. "Did that work?"

"Not at all," I replied, "and it's not my style so I had a hard time looking anything but foolish. The next time my car needed servicing, I scheduled an appointment with the service manager and asked, 'Do you have a wife? Mother? Aunt? Grandmother? Female cousin? Sister? Or daughter?' 'Yes,' he stammered, looking at me strangely and probably wondering if I was a crazy woman. "Then you know how unsettled a woman can feel when her car isn't working properly, or when it's not road safe and, most especially, when she feels she's been overcharged. Right?'"

"Oh," said, Tina. "I wouldn't want to admit that. Nor play the 'poor me' role. We women should just learn to do some things ourselves."

"Tina," I said, holding up my hands for her inspection. "Look at my beautiful fingernails. Can you see me changing spark plugs?"

"No," she laughed, "but I still think women should know the basics of auto repair."

"Oh, give me a break, Tina!" I said. "It's not the basics that's the problem. For example, I once took a course on how to change a tire. You know what? In my life I've had only one flat tire, and I can tell you it was quite a pleasant experience."

"Really," Tina asked, looking at me as though I was confused. "How so?"

"When I realized that quite possibly my tire was flat, I pulled over to the side of the road and a Chippendale dancer on his way to work stopped to help!"

Astounded, Tina laughed. "No way!" she mocked.

"Honest. I'm not kidding! And he gave me a door pass to see his evening performance."

"No! Did you go?" she asked wide-eyed.

"Absolutely, are you kidding!" I replied.

"Honestly, Bettie," she said, "you have all the luck. It'd be my luck to have the radiator blow up or have one of those million little rubber hoses go astray. Worse, no one would stop and the highway assistance call box would be miles away!"

"That's funny!" I said, laughing.

"No, it's not," she countered tersely. "That's why I think everyone should know the basics under the hood," she badgered.

"There are no *basics* under the hood, Tina," I said, thinking she might be underestimating the complexity of mechanics. Looking at her earnestly, I tried again, "Tina, have you ever cleaned a chicken or a bird of any kind?"

"Unfortunately, yes," she replied, giving me a weird look.

"Well, I have, too. When I look under the hood of my car, it reminds me of the heap of entrails pulled from the chicken being prepared for dinner."

"Oh my Lord," she said. "You're a case. Okay, okay, your point's well taken. So tell me, then what happened? How did you leave it at the service shop?"

"I said to him, 'If you were responsible for servicing your daughter's car, I believe you would take every precaution to make absolutely sure it was road safe, and the cost of service would reflect an honest estimate. I want you to service *my* car as though it were your daughter's. I often travel long distances at night, and it sure would be comforting to know I had a reliable dealership that serviced my car with the utmost attention to detail and concern for my safety, and that the service was affordable."

"Wow," said Tina. "That took moxie."

"It worked," I said. "I've been going to this service shop for nearly eight years, and I'm really happy with them. Every time I go in there, the manager comes out and greets me personally. And I always ask about his daughter!"

"Okay. I get your point," Tina said. "My plan of action is Plan B."

"Plan B for Bouncer?" I teased.

Tina chuckled. "Bouncers . . . bouncers . . ." She rolled her eyes, one finger tapping the side of her cheek. "Hmmm, I don't know any! Let me think, let's try the category of bouncer material . . ." Suddenly, she sat up, snapped her fingers and shrieked, "I've got it! I know just who to ask: James!" Her smile of glee grew wider. Narrowing her eyes in a vindictive yet playful scowl, she said, "Now there's a man who loves to take on a cause! Tomorrow, James and I are going to call on Nick in his office. Want to come?"

"Sure," I said.

"That's strange," Tina said with a perplexed look on her face. "The office door locked during business hours?" She knocked vigorously on the door to the office where she had worked for more than two years. There was no response. "I know that's his car," she said. Then James knocked, but not as she had. This time the door rattled and clanged from the force of his pounding. Still, there was no response.

"I know that's his car," Tina repeated. "Maybe he left with someone." Noses pressed to the glass and hands cupped around our faces to prevent the reflection on the glass as we peered in, the three of us strained to see if anyone was inside.

There was no sign of life.

Baffled, we stood for a moment on the steps of the building. "What do you want to do now, Tina?" her companion asked.

"I don't know. I feel so bad that I've asked you to come all the way here with me to help collect my money, only to find no one in the office. It's odd that he's not here. He always gets to the office early. It's almost 9:30 and tomorrow is D-day for the Hellman account, an account that determines the future of this company."

In unison, we all peered in, searching once again for someone inside. That's when we saw him peek from his office door down the hallway.

He knew we had seen him. He was caught.

"I'll bet that rat thought we had left by now," Tina said sarcastically as she waved and smiled sweetly to the man inside who was now forced to deal with the three people at the door.

He unlocked the door from the inside and opened it. "Oh, hi Nick!" Tina greeted him, as though she wasn't aware he had deliberately holed up in his office.

Though she had liked her job, she wasn't going to miss working with Nick. Tina disliked being made executor of Nick's deliberate cover-ups. Now *she* was subjected to his dishonesty. Tina had been tracking Nick down for over a month in an effort to collect her money. He knew it and had installed an infinite array of ploys—from evasion (by phone and in person), to promises of the check being in the mail. Not receiving her check triggered a chain reaction of late payments on her bills. Furthermore, it ate into valuable time needed to look for new employment and took precious time away from her teenage daughter. It resulted in negative feelings toward the company. Even if she wasn't fond of Nick, she had enjoyed her work and admired the other general partners in this small operation. In a nutshell, she didn't need the hassle.

"Oh," Nick said casually. "What a surprise to see you."

I'll bet it is, I thought.

"Come in, come in," he instructed.

Artfully, Tina introduced us. The men disliked each other instantly.

"Been busy?" Tina asked, hoping the small talk would bridge the gap between professional demeanors and the obvious ocean of uncomfortable feelings swimming around in the room.

"Sure have. It's been a chaotic time," Nick responded, leading us into his office.

"I'm glad things are looking up for you. I came by to pick up my check," Tina said. We sat down across from Nick, who was now behind his messy desk shuffling a stack of papers.

"Your check?" he asked, feigning surprise. "You should have received it by now."

"Yes, I should have, but I haven't," Tina said assertively. Stirring through the documents on his desk once again, Nick said, "It doesn't seem to be here. Did you fill out an hours form?" Tina listened with detached disgust as he offered up idle excuses as he had done countless times before. "Oh, yeah, I seem to remember that the accountant said he needs to have you fill out some other form," Nick said. "Why don't you fill out another hours form and I'll ask that the check be ready for you tomorrow." Nick was smiling now, genuinely pleased with his latest invention. With tolerant restraint, we sat listening to Nick babble on about his East Coast partner dissolving their partnership and the legal mess he was in.

"I need to get paid today for the hours I've already worked," Tina reiterated, bypassing the excuses unrelated to her missing paycheck.

Nick shuffled through his messy desk once again, as if looking for the mysterious form.

"Nick, this has gone on too long—beyond my waiting any longer," Tina stated with a calm she now struggled to maintain. "I need to be paid today."

"Oh, I understand, but the accountant . . ."

Perhaps deciding it was time to come to the rescue of the damsel in distress, James interrupted, "Pay her today, out of your own pocket if you have to. You can take it up with the accountant later." This he said with an air of calm authority.

Nick's shuffling sped up. He agreed with anxious resignation, "I guess I could do that. It's not standard procedure, I know I saw the form."

With quiet confidence, James stood up, folded his arms across his chest and said, "You look like you're a decision-maker. You're obviously in charge here. Just pay her." Then, articulating each word slowly, he repeated, "Just . . . pay . . . her."

Nick looked around superficially, then opened a drawer and pulled out a notebook of checks. "Oh well, forget the form. Let the accountant be mad at me—everyone else is," he sniveled. He wrote out a check. "Here," he said handing the check to Tina, "that should do it then."

Tina looked at the check, written for less than she was owed. "This doesn't represent the full amount that you owe me," she stated.

Twisting the facts, Nick said, "If I remember correctly, there was some sort of settlement agreement."

"This isn't what is owed me," Tina responded, giving him no time to fabricate the final amount of the check.

"Well, you'll have to take it up with the accountant," Nick said, still trying to postpone the inevitable.

Once again Tina's stand-in bouncer took over, "Pay her what she is owed. Today. Now. Let's stop the nonsense."

"No, no," Nick's voice thinned as he whined. "I'm not trying to be a shyster. Okay, okay, let me see that." He all but grabbed the check from Tina's hand and wrote out a new one.

Handing her the new check, he said, "Here you go, then."

"Are you all right with it now, Tina?" James asked.

"Yes," she said.

Nick exchanged polite good-byes with Tina and me, but the men had dispensed with social niceties. Neither said anything to the other.

As we were leaving, Nick called out, "You know, Tina, I really liked your work. Things should be picking up around here again in the not-too-distant future. If you are ever looking for a job . . ."

Tina could hardly believe what she was hearing. Looking appalled, she stopped, turned to face him and said, "Thank you, but no thank you. If you are interested in the reasons why, we can conduct an exit interview where we can discuss and document the integrity issues that prevent me from returning to work for you. Shall we arrange that?" Tina stood her ground and waited for a response.

Nick was silent.

A few minutes later, we climbed into the car. "I think you handled it very well," I said to her.

"Well, I'm grateful you both came along. Your being there really bolstered my self-confidence and gave me the courage to stay in that frame of mind rather than get nasty with him," Tina said. "I really had to bite my tongue to keep myself from giving Nick a piece of my mind. When he said I was welcome to come back once the company got up and rolling again, I so wanted to say, 'I know your wife is looking for a job. You might think about hiring her. Maybe she'll be better equipped to handle your hostile personality and your poor ethics and won't depend on her paycheck as much as I do.'"

"Why didn't you?" James asked.

"Why lower my standards? It wasn't worth it. When dealing with people like Nick who have little regard for ethics and integrity, it can be tempting to stoop to their level and play by their rules. But why do it?"

"He'll suffer the consequences of his unfit behavior sooner or later," James said trying to console her. "What goes around comes around."

"Well, at least Plan B worked," Tina declared. Looking at me she said, "Thanks for being there with me. It helped me maintain integrity instead of resorting to acting from my fear of being put off once again."

"You're welcome," I said. "Malcolm Forbes once said, 'To measure a man is to measure his heart; integrity, honor and principle is a good place to start.' It'd be nice if we didn't have to deal with people like Nick, but the fact of the matter is, we do. In an ideal world, you wouldn't have to resort to a Plan B to collect something rightfully owed you. The true victory here is that you successfully faced a person without integrity while still maintaining your own."

"And you did, Tina," said James. "You should be proud of yourself. Your example spoke loudly. Perhaps the only way to improve things is to look within and measure our actions against our own standards."

"Perhaps," said Tina, coming from her heart as she always does, "Nick just needs others to show him how to get in touch with his heart."

She may be right. Perhaps the heart, like people, is more in need of a model than a critic.

15 The Heart of Christmas

*Never forget that the most powerful
force on earth is love.*

—Nelson Rockefeller

The man read the church bulletin announcing that the congregation was aware that one of their families was experiencing hardship and could afford neither Christmas gifts for their children nor food for a traditional holiday celebration. Members of the congregation were encouraged to donate food, gifts and whatever else they could. The bulletin asked that members of the congregation bring all donations to the church by six that afternoon. Everyone would then form a caravan and deliver the goods to the family. Nudging his wife who sat in the pew beside him, he pointed to the pamphlet and whispered, "We *must* help."

Scanning the announcement, she nodded in agreement and returned a whispered, "Yes."

On the way home, the couple told their children what the bulletin had announced and discussed what their family could do to help. It was agreed: they would spend the day collecting toys and food and other items for this family in need. With that plan of action, they set out.

Each family member was warmed by helping someone in need, especially during a season of "giving." The couple and their three young sons hurried to the church to deliver everything they had gathered.

Once at church, they were both surprised and pleased to find so many other families participating in what the father had called "the heart of Christmas." Headed by the pastor and his family, cars and minivans loaded with an assortment of items—food, clothing, even a Christmas tree—lined up to begin the trip to the family who needed the congregation's outpouring of love, donations and sense of community. Like the others, this family took their place in the procession and set out to deliver "Christmas."

Several minutes into the trip, they were surprised to find themselves on their street. Within minutes, the cars in front of them drove into the driveway of *their* home.

They were the family in need and the recipients of the congregation's outpouring of love and support. And its Christmas heart.

16

Have You Ever Talked to an Angel?

All I have seen teaches me to
trust all I have not seen.

—Ralph Waldo Emerson

We were on our usual Saturday morning three-mile run, four friends and colleagues each meeting at various points along the way. William and Connie began at the same starting point, I joined them next, and within a quarter of a mile Deborah completed our group. As usual, a conversation was in progress when I joined the jaunt.

"So, have you ever actually *talked* to an angel?" Connie asked William.

"Not exactly *talk*, like we're talking now, but yes, I have."

Now turning the bend and about to head up into the canyon, Connie quickly glanced at me before bowing her head to focus on the uneven terrain beneath her feet. "And you?"

"Mmhmm," I replied.

"Wow! Did this conversation leap from the everyday to the ethereal with one simple question, or what?" she laughed nervously.

"How's that?" I asked, wondering what she wanted to clarify.

"It's just too far out for me. I'm into practicality. I mean, my main concern in life is to support myself and my kids. It's a constant struggle to juggle the needs of children, meet the demands of my job and then find time for myself. I could use a nanny, a bigger income and some sleep. The idea that my life could be better by asking for help from a feminine form in a diaphanous gray robe borders on the desperate," Connie replied.

"Desperate?" I queried, wondering if she considered guidance a gesture of strength or weakness.

"Okay, mystical then," she said.

"I don't think of angels as shimmering mystical creatures, Connie," I said. "I think of angels as a *force*, a dynamism of guidance, offering me a *pure* form of thought, one that I may not derive on my own. Kind of like the $1 + 1 = 3$ theory. For me, angels are an omnipotent support system, a divine gift sent to help me as I go about my life, mine for the asking."

"See!" Connie badgered. "This is why I have such a hard time with the whole notion. It's all too heady for me. Besides,

Bettie, I can't think of anyone who 'has it together' more than you do. Why do you need guidance from anyone?"

"Thanks for the glowing review, Connie," I laughed, "but believe me, no one can muck up my life more than I can. It's not that I need *an* angel, I need a force of them, full-time. Trust me."

"Well," she said, "it's just too religious for me."

"Perhaps the subject of angels wouldn't be so ethereal or so astonishing if we talked more often about *examples* of their work, you know, their intervention in our everyday lives," I said. "If we did, we would operate less from ignorance, and we'd be less fearful and skeptical. Then, by developing faith in their role in our lives, we'd have the miraculous assistance and protection they provide." I hoped my response wasn't too cumbersome. I knew she was looking for simplicity, not a dissertation.

Revealing her frustration, Connie said, "I'm just not on the same page as you guys are on this one, and yet, you know how much I respect and honor your work, your experiences and your friendships. You must know something I don't."

Though we were uniquely different and vibrant personalities, we were good friends. Ours was a relationship best described as a kinship, based on mutual regard and esteem. Over the years we had been a sounding board for the wondering and wandering in our lives. We coped with spouses in mid-life change or in job crisis; questioned the best ways to raise active, growing, curious children; grew our businesses while aligning them with our own natures; puzzled out the meaning and purpose of our own lives; and, like everyone, struggled to balance all the things in our lives. Quite frankly, Connie's doubting of angels surprised me, yet I knew this sort of questioning was a part of the path toward growth and acceptance.

"Are you having difficulty believing that angels communicate with us mortals," William asked her, "or is the notion of angels unbelievable? Let me ask you, do *you* believe in angels?"

Connie hesitated before answering, "Truthfully, I can't say that I do, but I can't say that I don't. I guess I could say that I believe in the *concept* of angels. But again, it's a tough one for me."

"At those times when you do believe," he prodded, "is it a personal experience or a nebulous one?"

"Oh, for sure it's nebulous," she said dogmatically, "as is the whole concept of being able to literally interact with an angel."

"I do think a lot of people identify angels in a whimsical fantasy context," I said, "such as the everyday tangible symbols that we put on top of a Christmas tree, bake into sugar cookies, wear as jewelry, use to decorate valentines or calendars, or set on our children's beds next to their teddy bears. And yet, I truly believe that, more and more, people are acknowledging the real work of angels as spiritual beings sent to guide, assist and protect us."

This was about the point where Deborah joined us. As usual, she was on time. "Hi, guys!" she said in her usual sunny disposition.

"Boy, am I glad you're here, Deborah," Connie greeted her. "We're discussing whether or not angels are more than a poet's fleeting fantasy and I'm feeling like a neophyte. Tell me, Deborah, do you believe in angels?"

"Absolutely. No question," Deborah responded as she adjusted her pace to meet ours. Connie groaned. "Hey, I can't say I became a believer overnight," Deborah added. "In fact, it took me awhile to understand not only what angels *were*, but why I was curious in the first place. Believe me, at first I felt a belief in angels belonged in the 'woo-woo' category because it was just a little too deep and mystical for me. I don't feel that way anymore. The evidence of angels in our midst is all around us."

"It's just a real stretch for me," our friend said. "I mean, *what is* an angel anyway?"

Deborah offered a simple reply. "A messenger."

"I know it deserves a certain amount of respect and reverence," Connie said, "but at the same time I need more concrete evidence. I mean, is there proof they exist? Sometimes I think it's just a modern day notion, the latest fad."

"Oh, Connie," I said, "it's much more than a fad. A number of religions accept the belief that there are, between God and mankind, various classes of intermediary beings called angels."

"Yeah," Deborah said. Citing Hebrews 13:2 she said, "Scripture says that 'many of us have entertained angels without knowing it.'"

"Wow, too much," Connie jeered. "How about proof? Like, *when* have any of you personally talked to an angel?"

By now we had come to the end of our run. Still knee-deep in our conversation, we did what we often did, we sat down and finished our talk.

William went first. "I'll give you an example," he said. "Last year when my wife filed for divorce, I was devastated. The day she actually removed her things from the house was the most intense pain I've ever known. As I was driving from work, it hit me that I was coming home to an empty house—literally. No wife, no kids, not even furniture. I pulled over to the side of the road and just cried. I begged for relief from my deep sorrow. Within minutes after I began driving again, I was the first on the scene of an accident. Here was an emergency situation where others desperately needed my help. It was nearly ten o'clock by the time I got home. I was so exhausted I could do nothing but sleep—something I hadn't done in weeks. The peace and relief I found while serving someone else relieved the momentary pain I felt. Incidences such as *receiving* what I need (not always what I want) happen to me all the time. You see Connie, for me, these are not just coincidences, but rather divine intervention directed to my needs. In the case of my being needed to help at the scene of the accident, it was an answer to my plea for a reprieve from my own anxious thoughts."

Disputing that notion, Connie said, "And that makes you a believer? I mean it could have been a coincidence."

"For me, experiences accumulate and increase my understanding and acceptance of divine intervention," William said. "They expand my perspective on the nature and work of angels."

"So if angels are helpmates, if they are sent to assist us," Connie questioned, "how do they communicate?"

"I think angels communicate with us in different ways,"

Deborah said. "We may call it intuition, instinct, a whisper of inspiration, a spirit appearing in a dream or in person, or something else entirely, but basically it's about revelations."

"But aren't we talking standard stuff?" Connie asked. "I mean, how do you differentiate an ordinary random dream from a message of inspiration?"

Sounding patient and fatherly, William answered, "For me, besides this overall feeling that what's going on is *special*—even *divine*—there's the vividness of the experience. Its message sets it apart from an ordinary dream. Plus, the dream doesn't fade from my memory as do the dreams that are a product of my mind's randomly selecting images from the business of my head. It's as if this dream has a clear message, one applicable to my life. I'm able to recount the details days, months, years later."

"But how do you decipher if an inspiration, or a dream for that matter, is given to you to guide your actions versus just to supply random information?" Connie asked. "Give me an example."

"For me," I said, "the element of doubt is removed. I question everything in life, but when I'm receiving divine guidance, nothing in me will doubt. The message is *that* clear."

"You see," Connie jeered. "These are all in your minds. There is no concrete evidence of angels existing in a form other than inspiration."

"Don't be so quick to dismiss it," William counseled. "I do think our experiences are personal, and I trust that for each of us, intervention will come in the most appropriate way and in accordance with the situation at hand. Though I often ask for peace of mind and emotional comfort, sometimes I'm *shown* guidance. For example, during my divorce, my wife on several occasions asked for increasing amounts of alimony and on each occasion was awarded more. There came a point where I was about to be financially devastated. Most of our assets were tied up in the house. My wife wanted to live with a man she met and wasn't particularly interested in having our three kids live with her. The idea of two parents living under two different roofs made our kids so sad. That she didn't want them to live full time with her added to their feeling rejected. I felt I should buy her out of the house and retain the home as a way to restore stability in our children's lives. There was a point where an increase to her alimony meant that there was no way I could afford the mortgage payments, her alimony and the financial needs of my children.

"Unfortunately, my soon-to-be-ex-wife was not at all interested in resolving the problem together. She simply wanted her share of the assets from the sale of the house. I was in such a quandary. Should I buy the family home or sell it? Every night, I went to bed wondering what I should do. Should I keep the house and hope that I could afford it? Should I sell it and lessen my monthly financial burden? I'd go to bed saying, 'Tomorrow I'll put the home up for sale.' Yet in the morning, I'd wake up and say, 'No, doggone it, I'm going to make this work.' Day after day this went on. I'd solve the problem each and every day, twice. Of course, on both occasions the resolution was different! One particularly sleepless night, I awoke to three angels in my bedroom. I thought for sure the stress had become too much. 'Come with us,' they said in unison. They led me to the south side of the house where a full cord of wood was piled, a purchase I made less than one week before. Immediately I thought, 'William, why would you buy enough wood to last all winter long if you thought you might put the house up for sale?' Next they led me into the office in my home, an office I had set up three weeks prior when I realized I was going to assume more of my children's day-to-day needs. On my desk was a business card with the name of a man I had personally met five days ago while waiting in my dentist's office. This man was known in the loan industry for his ethical, compassionate and exceptional ability to help those in divorce open and close a loan—when the odds seemed against it. Next to the card was a balance sheet on which I had tallied all the ways I could reduce the monthly expenditures. All these actions pointed to my knowing that I would be staying in the family home. As an example, I had closed my post office box and changed all my mail delivery to my home. I had done this not more than two weeks prior. After taking this inventory, I walked to my children's rooms and I glanced at their peaceful faces. I knew for certain they would be sleeping in these very beds, in these very rooms they loved so much, until they had graduated from high school. I closed my eyes. There was only one answer to the question of whether I should buy or sell the family home. Just as the angels showed me, my children and I were to make our way forward. The family home would be our point of healing and recovery. From that moment on, it was easier."

Needing more proof, Connie asked, "Did you actually *see* these angels or were they symbolic?"

"These were very real," William told her. "Either that or the impression was so strong I could see the mental pictures and hear words that helped me understand the message."

Quieted by William's tale of his passionate experience, Connie simply responded, "Wow."

"What comes to mind for me," Deborah said without prompting when Connie looked to her, "is an experience I had at our family reunion last year. I try to stay sensitive to what I described earlier as that still, small voice. It's a voice I have come to recognize and treasure. The family reunion was one occasion when the voice was not the same as usual. In fact, I feel strongly that the angel who spoke to me that day was my grandmother who had passed away several years earlier. The voice and manner were so distinctively hers, I recognized them almost immediately."

"What did she say to you?" I asked with fascinated curiosity.

"It's a long story but in a nutshell she let me know it was important for one of my younger cousins to be at the family reunion. Due to extenuating circumstances, I was about the only person who could help her get there. The morning of the reunion, family from all over the United States—and even a few living abroad—had flown into San Diego and were gathering for an all-day beach party less than a half-hour's drive from my home. As I was getting my six-week-old baby and the rest of my children ready for a day of fun, I heard a soft but distinct voice ask, 'What about your cousin, Summer? Where's Summer? She should be with the family.' I dismissed these words with the thought that I was lucky my kids and I were able to go. Packing a newborn with all the necessary paraphernalia (playpen, diaper bag, bottles, umbrella, blankets, beach chair, towels and so on) up and down a steep rocky cliff—not to mention my four other kids—was going to be no small feat. Still the voice persisted. It asked me to find Summer and make sure she got to the reunion. I finally gave in to the prompting and telephoned. I discovered that Summer's mother was working and 11-year-old Summer didn't have a way to make the 30-mile trip. Unfortunately, my car was in the shop and I was carpooling with some other family members. I didn't see a way for me to help. Yet the voice persisted and seemed to get louder and louder in a style that was distinctly my grandmother's.

"As I was getting everything situated on the sand after arriving at the beach, I found myself mentally arguing. I reminded my angel grandmother that I'd called. Summer didn't have a ride and there wasn't anything more I could do. Finally my angel grandmother simply said, 'Go and get her.' 'How can I go and get her? I don't even have my car here?' I countered. 'Borrow one,' she replied. 'My parents have two cars here, I guess I could borrow one of theirs,' I thought. 'What about the baby? There's plenty of people who can look after the older kids, but what about the baby?' I pleaded. 'I'll take care of the baby. Everything will be fine. You go and get Summer,' my angel grandmother reassured me.

"I can hardly describe the incredible peace and calm that filled me as these words were spoken. I intuitively knew that all my children would be well cared for while I went to pick up Summer. My parents lent me their car. They also offered to watch my children. My sister sat in a beach chair next to the baby, who fell asleep on a blanket under an umbrella.

"The hour-and-a-half round trip to pick up Summer was uneventful, except for the incredible feelings of joy I felt as Summer talked glowingly about the past family reunions she attended with Grandma and Grandpa, before Grandma died. She recounted the fun trips to various reunions over the last couple years in the motor home with Grandpa and some of our other cousins. I knew the situation in her immediate family had been turbulent over the past year, and now realized why it was so important for Summer to attend this reunion and feel the support and love of her extended family.

"When Summer and I reached the beach, all was well. Amazingly, the baby—who was a bit colicky and normally would have only taken a short half-hour nap—had slept peacefully the entire time I was away. As I sat down next to my sleeping baby, I watched Summer run and greet a few of her cousins playing in the surf. Once again I heard my angel grandmother's voice say, 'You see, everything is fine here. Thank you, oh, thank you.' I knew in my heart that somehow my baby's unusually long nap was not just a coincidence. When I think back on that extraordinary day, I have a mental image of my infant daughter sleeping soundly on the beach under an umbrella, tended by my angel grandmother. It's an image I'll never forget."

Another thoughtful silence followed Deborah's story, as we each digested her words. Finally Connie broke the silence by asking, "Do you believe that angels talk to every-one or just a select few?" She was looking in my direction as she asked this. Assuming she wanted to hear my thoughts on it, I answered, "I believe that a primary role for angels is that they are directed to carry out a response to our prayer. And yes, I believe that everyone who asks for help or guidance receives it. It's been said that prayers reach heaven as beams of light, and that organized groups of angels answer each prayer. Supposedly, the brighter beams are answered first because they represent the most sincere and heartfelt requests. A special priority is given to a mother's selfless prayer for her child."

"So, you think we can ask for help on behalf of someone else?" Connie asked.

"Yes," I said. "I think angels' work includes being sent to guide, protect and comfort our loved ones when we pray for their well-being. Scripture has it that a mother's prayers on behalf of her children always find a home in God's heart, and that those beams get first and immediate attention. I believe this is true. I've experienced this firsthand, both from my own mother and with my daughter. For example, my mother and I are very close. I always know when she's thinking of me, most especially when she is worried about me or missing me. On those days when my heart is heavy or my life becomes a bit overwhelming, I literally feel my mother's prayers for me and my family. There have been times when I feel surrounded by the peace and comfort of angels. At these times, I know that my mother has had a loving hand in this. I distinctly recall once standing at a window in my home succumbing to my sadness over a particular situation. An enormous decision I was about to make weighed heavy on me. I felt so vulnerable, so alone, so tender. Suddenly a dense pocket of benevolent warmth enveloped me. It was as though I was a child wrapped safely in the bosom of my mother, a feeling of being totally tended to. It was such a comforting feeling that my sadness disappeared, replaced by a feeling of strength, peace and calm. I called my mother and she said, 'I've been thinking about you today and praying for you.'

"My mother has this same intervening bond with my daughter. Though my mother and I are very close, she and my daughter are soulmates. Their bond belongs to the two of them, and I wouldn't pretend to know of its past and future history or the depth of its possibilities. As a mother who dearly adores and cherishes her child and wants the very best for her, I feel lucky that my mother and she are so close, but I know that luck doesn't cover the magnitude of what they have. So, I just accept it and feel peaceful with it. I know that my daughter has an anchor of strength via my mother. I know that my mother has prayed for the well-being of my daughter. I truly believe that my daughter receives blessings on my mother's behalf.

"The answering of our prayers, our quandaries, our hearts' needs is such a treasured thing. It is an enormous solace to me as a mother that each day my daughter faces the world, my prayers for her health, safety and well-being are heard and acknowledged. I know that my daughter feels my love for her through my prayers on her behalf. There have been many occasions when I've prayed for her and know that she has been sent help guided by angels.

"And, I am comforted that angels will carry out her requests as well. As an example, three years ago I went away for a couple of days on a planned ski vacation. During the second day of the trip as I was sitting on the gondola on my way up the mountain, my heart registered an ache I'll never forget. Intuitively, I *knew* this pain was my daughter needing me. I immediately skied to the lodge and called my answering machine. There I heard my daughter's crying voice: she had been taken to the hospital with a soccer injury. My heart had been contacted so that I could be responsive to my daughter's needs.

"See, for me, it's easy to believe, *because* I believe. Goodness knows I could never have done this alone. I've experienced so much love and joy and support—even amidst trials and tribulations—I've been guided in my life and so protected from getting into harm's way, that I must acknowledge a *source*. I believe in mankind, but I also know that, left to our own devices, most of us would never be able to experience the fullness of the worlds available to us. I do think that much of this love is ushered in on the wings of angels."

Again there was a respectful stillness among us. Finally Connie broke the silence by continuing her interrogation, one that now carried a much more gentle and accepting tone. "Do you think each of us are assigned a specific guardian angel?" she asked.

"You know Connie, I'm not really sure. I've come to recognize a familiar positive and gentle inner voice that seems always to be close at hand. Maybe that's my own guardian angel," I responded. "At other times, I may not understand who or what provides specific intervention. I'm trying to get better at filtering out the negative noise that sometimes keeps me from hearing the subtle promptings. I'm just trying to learn and do what feels most right."

"I agree with that," Deborah said, "although my own experience leads me to believe that there may be a host at hand, what I playfully call the Grandstand Theory."

"Oh, do explain, Deborah," I said, really wanting to know. I love Deborah's tantalizing sense of humor.

"I have this picture in my mind of going through life with a grandstand full of angels cheering me on," she said. "It's amazing how easy it is to pass by some of life's temptations when you feel a crowd of angels are watching. At those times I'm out of integrity or go off in a negative manner, it's almost as if that same crowd moans in unison, like you'd hear at a baseball game!"

We all laughed. "What a great concept," I said. "I could use a grandstand of angels to look out for me!"

"Oh, please elaborate," Deborah said laughing.

"Not on your life!" I said.

"I wish I had all the answers as you all do," Connie sighed.

"You know, Connie," I said, "I don't have all the answers. But I think it's more simple than we think. Angels love us and look after us. They talk to us through our hearts and minds. If we recall the miracles—big and small—that we've each experienced in our lives and ask ourselves if angels were involved, we might come closer to acknowledging their work. Just as you do, I still have questions."

"For instance?" she asked.

"I often wonder if being an angel is an obligation or a reward. I question why it is that children easily believe in angels, whereas adults are prone to doubt. And I want to know how to become more sensitive to recognizing the influence and prompting of angels at work in my life, stuff like that."

"Well," Connie said softly, "Something sure is running interference in my life right now."

"Connie," I said, "My father once said to me, 'All the truths you'll ever need exist in your heart.'"

"I'm starting to believe that," she said.

When a Father Says "I Love You"

Love is the key to life, and its influences
are those that move the world.

—Ralph Waldo Trine

As a child, selecting a Mother's Day gift for my mother was always easy: a box of candy, a bouquet of picked flowers, a lovely card with a heartfelt verse. No matter what size the box of candy, what pedigree the flowers or what color the card, she always expressed surprise and gratitude. But a gift for Dad on Father's Day—now, that was more difficult. "What do you want for Father's Day, Dad?" I would ask. "I know you don't want flowers or candy. What would you like?" His answer was the same one he gave when I asked him what he wanted for his birthday. And for Christmas. And on Valentine's Day. "Oh, I don't need anything," he would reply nonchalantly. I wanted so badly to say, "Well, maybe *you* don't, but *I* do. I want you to tell me—in words for once—that you love me. I *know* that you love me, but I want to *hear* you say it."

Because my father was such an all-powerful person in my life and because as a child I was too timid to say this to him, I didn't. Instead, one year I bought him a red plaid flannel shirt—one so lovely that it cost nearly $10\frac{1}{2}$ weeks of my carefully saved allowance. That was nearly 25 years ago.

Home on a family visit recently, I found myself sitting on my parents' bed, chatting with my mother as she cleaned their closet. Her approach was an interesting one: She'd reach into the closet, fetch a garment and hoist it into mid-air for inspection. It took mere moments for her to decide if the item went back into the closet or made its way to the pile of giveaways now mounting on the floor.

Out came a tattered shirt—in terrible condition. The shirt was faded; the elbows had patches on top of patches; the collar and sleeve cuffs were badly frayed; the neckline was completely worn through; few buttons matched; and the faded fabric was so antiquated that it hung limp and lifeless on the hanger.

Mother quickly hung it back in the closet.

Curious, I asked, "Mom, why did *that* shirt make its way back into the closet?"

"Oh, this darned old thing," she said, rolling her eyes. "It's not even fit for a dust cloth! Your dad doesn't wear it, of course, but he would ask me where it was if it were missing. I don't know what it is about that old thing," she said, and in a spirit of fun added, "it's just one of your father's many quirks."

"Mom," I asked, "do you remember anything about that shirt?"

"Not a thing," she said dispassionately. "I don't even remember patching it, though that's my stitching, all right. When I ask your father why he keeps it around, he says, 'Oh, I don't know.'"

"I want it," I said, "I'm going to ask Dad if I can have it."

"Well, don't get your hopes up," she said laughing. "He won't part with it."

I won't part with the memory of it.

One evening my five brothers and sisters and I were doing the evening chores. Within moments, I was having stomach cramps. Soon the pain was fierce. At first it felt like a blender at high speed, chopping around inside my stomach. Then it worsened. As the excruciating pain became more intense, the interval between spasms shortened. My parents put me to bed with a warm water bottle. Still, nothing could tame the savage war inside me. When it was apparent the acute pain was not going to subside, my parents took me to the emergency room at a local hospital. Within minutes I was wheeled into surgery for an emergency appendectomy.

As I stirred from the sedation and moaned in pain, I felt the soothing presence of my parents beside me. "We're right here with you," my mother said as she stroked my face and brow. "We love you," my father said, stroking my hair, "I love you." Not even the remaining Demerol in my bloodstream could drown out the addendum my father had added to the proverbial "we." It was the first time he had *spoken* these words to me. The importance I had assigned to hearing these words from my dad crystallized the moment and made everything about it memorable. I noticed that my parents looked tired, no doubt from standing guard throughout the late-night surgery and then in the recovery room. They looked concerned, but relieved. I noticed other things, too, like *the* red plaid flannel shirt my father was wearing—a gift to him from me that Father's Day.

"Mom," I said, watching as she continued sorting through clothes, shoes and other items, "why does it take some fathers so long to feel comfortable telling their children that they love them—to actually say the words, 'I love you'? What is it about those eight letters—three simple little words—that's so difficult for so many men to master?"

Looking thoughtful, she offered, "Sometimes it takes men a long time to use these words with the women they love, too." Then in a more lighthearted manner, she added, "You know the old joke—on their 50th wedding anniversary the woman asks her husband, 'Do you love me? You never tell me.' 'I told you I loved you on the day we were married,' he says to her. 'If the status had changed, I would have let you know.'"

Laughing, I said, "Mom, that's funny, but terrible, too."

My mother's comment caused me to recollect the relationship my parents shared, or at least my childhood sense of it. "Mom," I said, "throughout my childhood, I remember you telling Dad all the time that you loved him. You two were always so passionate with each other, I just assumed he told you he loved you all the time, too, even though I never heard him say it. Plus, I was with him on many of the occasions when he bought you perfume for Valentine's Day. And Christmas. And on your birthday! Speaking of perfume, did you get tired of only getting Chanel? I'd say, 'Dad, why don't you get her something else for a change?' and he'd say, 'She loves this perfume and I'm sure she's just about out of it.'" As Mom and I laughed at Dad's customary ritual, she reached up into the closet and brought down a box containing seven bottles of the same fragrance. "They do mount up!" Mom said, laughing.

"Is it really your very favorite perfume?" I asked.

"No, but it's his favorite!" she replied. Her seductive, all-encompassing smile and twinkling eyes told me that there was more to tell, and that I didn't have a right to it.

Wanting to explore the father-child relationship a bit more with this wise woman I love so much, I said, "Mom, three months ago I did an author's seminar and book signing for my *Values from the Heartland* book at Warwick's Books in La Jolla. One of the men in the audience asked me what I would be working on after the *Values* book. I got to talking about my new book and in particular, a story on fathers. This prompted me to ask for a show of hands from the men in the audience as to how old they were when they first remembered their fathers telling them that they loved them."

There must have been 40 or so men in the audience of about a hundred people. Of all the men who were over 45, none remembered ever having heard these words from their fathers. Incredible, isn't it! All had tears in their eyes when they admitted this was so. Only six men could remember their fathers telling them they loved them. Of these, one man said to me, "I was 44 years old when my father finally told me he loved me. It was the second most important day in my life." As though to distract himself from the pain of the memory, he forcefully swirled the nearly half-empty glass he held until the water whirled to the brim, as he added in a soft and tender voice, "I was shocked, taken by surprise. My father's words were so sacred to my heart that all I could do was turn away from him and cry."

Feeling genuinely sorry for the obvious hurt this man was still feeling, I said, "I'm sure your father loved you, even if he didn't say so in words."

"Because he didn't *say it,*" the man countered, "I felt he didn't. I never wanted to be a father myself because for me, being a kid was not all that great of an experience. And yet, I had all the things that kids are supposed to have—the Easter Bunny, Santa Claus, birthday presents. All arrived on cue. We lived in a good neighborhood, I went to a nice school, had friends—you know, all the right stuff. Even so, a big piece was missing."

So I asked him, "Did you ever consider that having all this stuff was at least a *sign* of your father's love?"

"It wasn't enough," he said matter-of-factly. "I needed to hear the words."

Then I asked, "Why do you think your father waited so long to say *I love you?*" Providing his father with a reason for his actions but not really addressing my question, he said, "My dad learned he was dying from cancer. I pined all my life to hear Dad say those words. Now that he's decided I'm worthy to hear them, he's no longer going to be around to say them."

"Have you become a father?" I asked.

"Yes," he said, "and I tell my 9- and 11-year-old each and every day that they are loved by their dad."

Recounting the story to my mother now as we sat on her bed, I said, "Mom, you should have seen how somber the audience became. Looking at everyone, I asked, 'Why do you feel that so many fathers don't readily say I love you?'" A man who looked to be about 40 responded, 'My father allowed my mother to represent him. It was sort of implied that they operated as a unit. A card or gift from *one* of them meant it was from the both of them. Even so, I've never excused my father from not buying a card (or present) himself or, at the very least, *signing* it himself.' This confession caused another man, one who said he never heard his father say the words directly, to say, 'That's just the way things are done. I'll bet it's not so different in many homes.'

"So once again I tossed it back to the group. 'Do you think that the majority of cards and presents parents give their children are signed, *Love, Mom and Dad* but purchased and signed by the mother?' Most all of the men nodded their heads yes. As I studied the crowd, I noticed that many of the women just stared straight ahead as if deep in thought. Some giggled nervously.

"'So if our mothers' actions stand for both Mom and Dad,' I badgered, 'why isn't that enough? Why do we children pine for . . .'

"Before I could finish my sentence, a man who had said he was 38 finished it for me. In a really cynical tone he asked, 'For the words from our fathers themselves?' He then proceeded to answer his own question: 'Because we want our fathers to represent *themselves*. Our mothers tell us they love us all the time and we think, "Yes, I know you do. But how about Dad?"'

"By now I wanted to know if other men shared a similar point of view or if this was an isolated case, so I asked this same question to groups throughout the country over the last several months. The responses are uncannily similar.

"It shouldn't be this way, Mom."

Patient and looking thoughtful throughout my discourse, Mom said playfully, "Oh, it's just another indication of the superiority of women, don't you think?" Though we laughed, my mother soon grew pensive. "In a mother's lexicon," she said, "*I love you* means many things, from simply, *It feels so good to be together with the both of us feeling good about each other*, like the feeling between you and me right now, to *I'm so pleased that you're in such a good place—happy, doing well, healthy, achieving, feeling purposeful*. It can mean *I'm happy for you* or *I'm happy about your current state of doing, being*. A mother places a high value on these things because they are signs that her children's hearts are in a state of prosperity, abundance. Perhaps mothers do use the words too lightly—if that's possible. And perhaps men don't use them enough, if that's really the case. Some men, like your father, never heard these words from their own fathers and were told to not let their hearts overrule their heads. Saying *I love you* was a sign the heart was leading and this was okay for women, but not for men. That aside, I do think that for many men, saying *I love you* is likely to be triggered by an experience."

"Like loss?" I asked, thinking about a comment from one man who had said, "My father's saying *I love you* was an admission of being mortal. He was gravely ill and felt he'd better say these words before it was too late."

"Mom," I said, "according to many of the men I talked with, by the time their fathers get around to saying 'I love you,' either the dad is old—very old—or recognizes that his children are. And many of these men felt that their fathers were more likely to say 'I'm proud of you' in place of 'I love you,' though even the words *I'm proud of you* were hard to come by. The son or daughter had achieved something on a grand scale, like graduating or receiving an award, or reached a milestone—like parenthood themselves—in order to hear it. And something else emerged that I found insightful. Most all of the men I talked with felt it was easier for their fathers to say *I love you* to their daughters than to their sons."

Looking thoughtful, Mom said, "It's changing. Your father *learned* to tell his children he loved them. And because he did, your brothers tell their children they love them all the time. But it's one thing to say it, another to show it. You can't discount the importance of actions as a means of expressing love, too. Making the necessary sacrifices to keep one's family healthy and together—even having two parents under the same roof—is no easy feat. These actions are as substantial as *saying* 'I love you.' There are children who are *told* by their fathers that they are loved, but the actions of these very men undermine the validity of these words. Deadbeat dads, for example. Assessing love, the value of words over actions, can be tricky. But I do hear what you're saying. Like you, I know how vital it is that fathers show *and tell* their children they love them. Perhaps we mothers need to help our sons know how very important it is that love be expressed in all ways."

I thought her point was a good one. "I agree, Mom," I said.

As I packed for my return trip to San Diego later the next day, I happened to glance out the window and spotted my father doing what I had watched him do on so many occasions. He was stooped over my (rental) car, the hood up, looking at the engine. I stopped to watched. First he checked the water level, then the oil. Then he wiggled each and every one of the many hoses, detecting if any were loose. He stood erect, closed the hood, retrieved his handkerchief from his pocket and polished the hood where he had touched it. He then walked in a full circle around the car, looking at the tires as he went. He kicked first the front left tire, then the front right tire, then the back right, and finally the back left. Apparently this last tire didn't pass the kick test because it was subjected to yet another kick. Dad then opened the car door, got in and looked over the gauges on the dashboard. When satisfied with whatever it was he was looking for, he started the engine. No doubt checking the brakes, he drove the car forward, then suddenly stepped on the brake. The car lurched to a stop. This same test was repeated as he put the car in reverse.

The scene was so touching, so familiar, that I had to laugh out loud. How I loved this about my father, the caretaker, the protector. He had managed to pick up the pieces of a life interrupted in times of war. He dreamed a big dream and put it in motion. His goals were to marry the woman he loved, own land, raise a family, keep them together, create financial security. Be a God-honoring man. He'd managed it all. Determined, self-disciplined. And an unquestionable guardian.

"Dad," I said, approaching him a few minutes later, "throughout my childhood I've watched you kick the tires on Mom's car every time she went somewhere. Over the years, I've watched as you do this to your grown children's cars, including my brothers, who are now in their 30s—and all of whom, I might add, are nothing short of master mechanics. You also kick the tires of all the grandkids who are driving. I don't need to ask you why you do this, but I would like to know what it means to you."

Deep in thought, he looked first at the ground and then at the car. "Oh, I don't know," he said, giving his customary explanation.

"Dad," I said, realizing that he wasn't going to offer a more profound reason, "I love it when you kick tires. It reminds me of how much you love and need your family. And speaking of love and need," I said, producing the red flannel shirt that I was holding in my hands behind my back, "I *love* this shirt and really *need* it. May I?"

Looking at the shirt brought a big smile to his face. "Oh, yeah," he said, eyes twinkling. "That was a pretty scary evening. For a moment there we thought we might lose you."

"No, Dad," I said, momentarily disappointed that his words that evening had been triggered by fear of loss. "I was just trying to scare you into saying 'I love you.' Do you remember telling me that evening that you loved me?"

Thinking it over, he said, "I do remember making a promise to God in exchange for your well-being."

"What did you ask for?" I asked.

"For your well-being," he said.

"What did you promise in return?" I asked.

Tenderly he explained, "As I was sitting in the waiting room that night of your surgery, I recalled being in the delivery room when you were born and getting to hold you when you were but moments old. Then suddenly you were 12. I realized that a lot of years had passed and wondered how they had gone by so quickly. I knew how much I loved all my children, and I wanted you kids to know it too."

"Dad," I said, loving and respecting this tender brute of a man, my trusted confidant and staunch friend, "I'm transferring this shirt from your closet to mine."

Tears came to his eyes as he said tenderly, "I've been saving it for you."

I was surprised at his words. "You have?" I asked, hoping he'd elaborate. He did.

"Funny at what we remember, isn't it? That night you were in surgery I recalled how excited you were as you watched me unwrap a gift you had given me for Father's Day. Obviously I didn't show as much enthusiasm as I should have because a look of sheer disappointment washed over your face. As I watched your labored breathing while you were in the recovery room, I kept praying that I wouldn't lose the opportunity to make it right."

"Dad," I said, "it's a cherished experience at the soul level to be *told* by your father that you're loved. But if you hadn't kicked those tires all those years, I would never known the *depth* and *breadth* of your words. Thank you for loving me so much—and for all of the ways your actions say it."

As I was walking back to the house, I heard the unmistakable gleeful squeals of my four-year-old nephew, Jared, as he bounded out of his parents' car. As soon as this vibrant little boy caught sight of his grandfather, he ran to greet him as fast as his little legs could carry him. Upon hearing the child's voice, a look of pure joy flooded my father's face. Though still some distance away, the little boy nevertheless reached out for his grandpa's hand. My dad extended his Herculean arms and tenderly scooped up his little grandson. A mammoth hand willingly sought the little hand begging to be touched. Ten fingers—long, strong ones and short, fine-boned ones—entwined affectionately. The exuberant child talked a mile a minute, nonstop, filling in Grandpa on the latest news in his exciting and busybody world. Adoration and devotion written all over his face, my father listened attentively, and smiled and nodded his head approvingly. When at last there was a pause in little Jared's animated chatter, my father said tenderly, "I love you, Jared." These words caused the little boy to turn his beaming young face and look squarely into his grandfather's eyes. "I love you, too, Gramps," he said, planting an unasked-for kiss on his grandfather's cheek.

My mother knew intuitively that you could never say *I love you* too much. My father had learned it.

Looking at the old shirt I held in my hands—a precious token, symbolic of my father's words and all the ways he showed them—I was reminded that for children young and old alike, parental love is a powerful anchor, offering untold support throughout our lives. One that none of us ever wants to give up. Nor the tokens that represent that it is so.

18

The Black Box

Love does not consist solely in gazing at each other but in looking outward together in the same direction.

—Antoine de Saint-Exupéry

I had just completed my presentation at the national conference. Noting the roster of speakers, many of whom were friends, I decided to visit a few. I stopped in a room nearby where my friend Dr. Harold Bloomfield, a renowned psychiatrist, was giving his seminar. Dr. Bloomfield's session had already begun. "How to Survive the Loss of Love" was the topic. Obviously it struck a chord; the large room was nearly filled. I located an empty chair near the front of the room and quietly took my seat.

"By a show of hands," Dr. Bloomfield began, "in the past year how many of you have experienced the loss of a pet?" Seated in the chair in front of me, a beautiful dark-haired woman raised her hand. She looked to be about 28 or 30 years old. "How about a job? Has anyone lost a job this year?" Along with others scattered throughout the room, she again raised her hand. Dr. Bloomfield continued, "Lost a close friend?" "Experienced the loss of personal property?" "A grandparent?" To each of these questions, the young woman raised her hand.

"How many here today have lost a marriage at some time during the year?" Again she raised her hand.

She isn't taking this exercise seriously, I told myself. No one that young, that lovely, and from all appearances that successful, could have so much personal tragedy all within a year.

At the conclusion of Dr. Bloomfield's poll, an older woman sitting next to me leaned forward, patted the young woman on her shoulders and whispered, "You're obviously in the right place, honey!"

Could it be so? I studied the youthful woman more closely. Here was a strikingly attractive, smartly dressed, meticulously groomed, physically fit and vibrant woman. Could she have already lost so much in life? The older woman raised her hand on the death of a pet and on the death of a spouse. She had lived nearly 40 years more than the younger woman.

The young woman was friendly and vivacious. Overhearing several of the comments she made, I could tell that she was witty, had a sense of humor and had an easy style of communicating. She also looked durable. If she lost a job, for example, certainly her combination of skills and personal assets would provide her with ample opportunities. Surely her career options must be wide open.

And who in his right mind would leave such an exquisite woman? How could he leave her when she was going through so much? Wouldn't he feel compassion and thus support her through such distressing and traumatic experiences?

Other questions surfaced. Aside from attending a public workshop intended to provide *insight*, was she getting individual counseling care or private therapy, perhaps? She would need to be diligent in her efforts toward recovery. Certainly her loss was expansive. It would take more than insight to work through loss and devastation of this personal nature.

Then I remembered Dr. Bloomfield's haunting last question: "How many have lost a child?" My own heart missed a beat at the mere thought of ever losing my precious daughter. Shoulders slumped, head lowered, the young woman in front of me had raised her hand on that one, too.

This wonderful woman is now one of my dearest friends. Her name is Renee, and she is all I've described and much more. We talk often of our lives and how we experience them, present and past.

"The sense of awakening I felt as I continued to raise my hand with each new question," Renee said, recalling that day, "allowed me to acknowledge the extent of the devastation I encountered in just one year." It wasn't until later that she experienced the depth, breadth and fullness of it all. It occurred to her that she better investigate how she had gotten here. "My life had bottomed out. I was in need of answers. What happened? Why? How could every aspect of my life change so drastically in just a 12-month period of time? If only I could foresee the answers to the deal-breaker questions: *What should I do? Where do I turn for advice? How do I prioritize everything?* Everything seems like it should be my first priority to me."

When surveying a crash site, investigators search the wreckage for the "black box" that contains the plane's flight data and cockpit voice recorders. This information can lead to the *what, why* and *how* of the disaster. As with any disaster, pinpointing what went wrong is crucial information: these sorts of mishaps must be prevented from occurring again.

Renee's search for her own personal black box meant she needed to go back to where her "flight" originated.

A successful businesswoman, wife and mother of three, Renee juggled a demanding travel schedule as a professional speaker with a bustling household. Her consuming responsibilities consisted of three young daughters, a husband, a five-bedroom house, several cars, a van, a boat, miscellaneous toys and a support staff of two to help maintain them all.

Her merry-go-round was in full swing when she discovered she was pregnant with her fourth child.

"I was thrilled with the news of my pregnancy," Renee said. "Just as my three previous ones had done, the news of a new baby rekindled personal feelings of joy, faith and hope in the future. Because each of the other pregnancies had been easy and my going to work each day actually enhanced my overall feelings of well-being, I didn't cut back on work this time either. Of course, I was by now in great demand in my work. I spent 12 to 16 days traveling cross-country each month!"

Like so many other families, her standard of living had risen to meet her income level. "I was head of the household," Renee said. "My husband took on the 'Mr. Mom' role, a position he cherished and had no intentions of giving up." As it turned out, he was all too eager for the family to maintain their present income level. This, he felt, was *her* responsibility.

Each trip to the airport stirred the rage building inside her for being forced to carry the family's financial load. Yet she continued to do so, denying the seriousness of the situation. That is, until she returned home from a four-day trip completely exhausted. The grueling schedule was taking a toll on her body. She visited her doctor. A sonogram showed a healthy growing baby, surrounded by an ominous build-up of tissue and clotting. Premature labor began in her 26th week of pregnancy. Within hours, it ended in a hospital emergency room—with the stillbirth of a baby boy.

"Words cannot describe the feelings of devastation and utter helplessness I felt," she said, her eyes filling with tears as she talked about her experience. "I looked at my new-born's small features, his perfect round head and his tiny lifeless body—a body that had grown within me. The sense of loss and pain surpassed any other I had ever suffered. It was as if life itself had left me along with my baby."

Still in a state of shock, Renee had to deal with questions she had never considered before, nor heard anyone else discuss. "'What name would you like to go on the death certificate?' the nurse inquired. 'Name?' I asked. The nurse said, 'I'm sorry for asking you to go through this, but we have to fill this out as soon as possible.'" Still tender from this harrowing experience, Renee shook her head sadly and continued, "There were other dire questions to address, too. All were as horrifying, if not more so. Like, 'What is to be done with the tiny body, cremation or burial?'"

This young woman had prepared herself for birth but had to confront death. "I found myself looking at the small coffin with its silk pillows and lining. I only wanted to accept that my baby son was just sleeping. Then I watched as they lowered him into his grave, and I knew that this single event would reshape my life forever."

Renee's investigation of her crash may never be completely over, though she has recovered the black box and learned from it. "When I sifted through the content, and listened to the record of the chain of events prior to my crash," Renee says, "I had to accept that a large share of the problem was caused by pilot error. When I took a close look at *me* and the ways in which I was living my life, I knew that not only was I the problem, but I was the *solution*, as well."

It was her turning point. It was then that she discovered the answer to the "king's three questions."

In his story, *The Three Questions*, Leo Tolstoy tells of a king who wants desperately to find the answers to these three questions: *What is the right time to do the right thing? Who is the right person to listen to? What affairs are the most important and need attention first?* He offers a great reward to any person who can answer them.

Many learned men came to the king and offered their advice. In reply to the first question, some said that in order to know the right time to do the right things, one must draw up a schedule in advance and strictly adhere to it. Others said that it was impossible to decide correctly the right time to do things, so the king should secure a council of wise men to help him determine the best time for everything. Others said there were some things which couldn't wait to be laid before a council. Instead they had to be decided immediately. In order to know whether or not to undertake them, one must know beforehand what was going to happen. Since only magicians would have these answers, one must consult magicians.

Equally various were the answers to the second question. Some said the king should listen most to those who were councilors. Others said the priests. Still others said the doctors or the warriors.

In response to the third question, some said it was science, others said it was skill in warfare, still others said it was religious worship.

All the answers were different, so the king gave the reward to no one. Still, he yearned to know the answers to the questions. He decided to consult a hermit widely renowned for his wisdom.

The hermit never came out of the woods where he lived all alone. He received no one but common folk. The king put on peasant's clothing and before reaching the hermit's abode, he dismounted from his horse, left his bodyguard behind and went on alone. When the king approached, the hermit—a frail and weak old man—was digging the ground in front of his hut. He greeted the king but went on digging.

"I have come to you, wise hermit," the king said, "to ask you three questions. What is the right time to do the right thing? Who is the right person to listen to? What affairs, or things to do, are the most important and need my attention first?"

The hermit listened, but gave no answer. He continued digging.

"You are tired," said the king, "let me take the spade and work for a while."

The hermit gave the spade to the king and sat down.

After digging for several hours, the king repeated his questions. The hermit again gave no answers, but rose, reached out for the spade and said, "Now rest awhile and let me work." The king didn't hand over the spade. Hour after hour passed. When it was nearly nightfall, the king implored, "I came to you, wise man, for an answer to my questions. If you can give me none, tell me so and I will return home." Suddenly, a man—his hands pressed against his bleeding stomach—came running from out of the nearby woods and, fainting, fell to the ground. The king quickly carried the injured man into the house, where he cleaned and bandaged the wound. Exhausted, the king lay down and fell fast asleep.

When the king awoke the next morning, he found the wounded man sitting at his bedside gazing intently at him. Seeing the king awaken, the wounded man begged for the king's forgiveness. "Why are asking for forgiveness?"

asked the king. "It is I who fell asleep while I should have been tending to your recovery."

"Dear king," began the man, "I knew you were going to see the hermit alone, and I had planned to kill you when you took leave of the hermit. When the day passed and you hadn't returned, I came out from where I had hidden in plans of ambushing you. Unfortunately for me, your bodyguard recognized me and wounded me in the battle that ensued. Oh, dear king," the man continued, "you have saved my life. Now, if you allow me my life, I will serve you as your most faithful servant and will bid my sons to do the same."

As you can imagine, the king was very glad to make peace with such an enemy. In fact, he not only forgave him, he sent his servants and his own physician to take the wounded man home and attend to him until he was healed.

The king then resumed his questioning of the hermit. "For the last time," pleaded the king, "I pray you to answer my questions, wise man."

"You have already been answered," said the hermit.

"How do you mean?" asked the king.

The hermit pointed out that had not the king taken pity on the hermit's weakness and helped him dig, the man would have attacked him as he had planned to do. Thus, the most important *time* was that spent helping the hermit dig the soil. In that moment, it was the hermit who was the most important *person*. Doing good by saving the intended killer's life was the most important *thing* to do—the business of the moment—for in this case, had the king not bound up his wounds, he wouldn't have made peace with an enemy. In this instance, the wounded man became the most important person, and what the king did for him was the king's most important business.

Of course the king was amazed by the simplicity of the insight: *There is only one time that is all-important—it is the present.* "The most necessary man is he with whom you are," teaches the hermit, "no man knows whether he will ever have dealings with anyone else. The most important affair is to do him good because for that purpose alone was man sent into this life."

Like the king, Renee has uncovered the answers to her three questions: The most important time is now. Doing what's important right now is the best way to leverage her time and efforts. The "answers" are within. Renee understands that much of the challenge is to always pay attention to the *voice within.*

Many things have changed in Renee's life as a result. "I discovered what was most important in my life," she said "and realized that I had to get current with it. For me, it was three young daughters. I also discovered what things I needed to change: my materialistic lifestyle and a marriage that wasn't healthy. I had to completely reorganize my life in a way that made it fulfilling to me and to those I love and care about.

"Now I find myself surrounded by love and an understanding of what true happiness is for me. What a gift this is!"

While not all of us face personal and outer devastation as Renee did, many of us do. Regardless of the extent of that loss, we are called upon to hear the pain and respond *lovingly*. This fosters an even deeper understanding, appreciation and acceptance of what we are going through. Furthermore, we must not give up. We must continue on our journey. Though feeling fragile or devastated, our hearts must go on without becoming bitter, closed or jaded.

This is never an easy task. It is always an arduous one, many times requiring that we seek assistance in deciphering the real clues in our "black box."

The good news is that our hearts *know* the answers to our three questions. It *knows* how truths exist personally for each of us. With an intuitive awareness and appreciation of the moment, it knows what people and activities are most important.

We must all promise to love ourselves enough to find our own truths and live them.

19 A Matter of Perspective

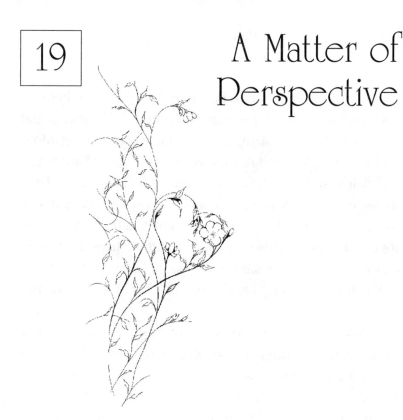

What force is more potent than love?

—Igor Stravinsky

I recently saw a cartoon in which a father, knee-deep in snow, tells his son that the snow drifts are nothing compared to when he was a child, when they piled as high as his chin. His son stands beside him, chin-deep in snow. Perhaps this says something about the change of perspective we acquire with time and maturity.

When I was a young girl, my family often went on Sunday "family" drives. I considered this one of the most boring activities I was required to participate in, primarily because it seemed too relaxed, leisurely and tranquil. The drives that consisted of flower gazing were the most excruciating. Mom and Dad would point out the colorful flowers blooming in the fields and meadows, in lovely neighborhoods. They drove ever-so-slowly past rows and rows of the outdoor blooms in the nearby town's greenhouse. If it wasn't for the ice cream cone promised at the end of these trips, I was sure all my brothers and sisters and I would have rioted.

We did complain. "This is boring!" one of us kids would say.

"Yes," the rest of us would chime in. From the front seat came the reply, "You may not appreciate the beauty of these lovely flowers now, but when you are older, you will." I was even more certain that being an adult must be pretty boring because my parents actually took great pleasure in these afternoon drives.

It wasn't that I had anything against flowers. My mother loved flowers and had planted them everywhere. Gorgeous purple and white morning glories climbed the siding on three sides of the house. Thick beds of marigolds added their coordinated hues of sienna brown, rust, orange and gold blooms to sheds and outbuildings. Pink and pale purple hollyhocks sprouted along the front of the barn, along the fences going down our half-mile-long lane and beside the big mailbox with the family name on it. I knew my mother loved flowers, and I considered her planting them everywhere one of her quirks and so accepted it. Being captive in a car looking at the flowers in other places was another matter.

When I first set up a home of my own as a young adult, my idea of plants were those that were potted and ready to be purchased either from grocery stores or street-side shops. Later on I graduated to enjoying fresh bouquets delivered by the local florist. I enjoyed my yard hassle-free, meaning that the neighbor boy was hired to cut the grass. The lawn went from one property line to the other, the only impediments were the neatly trimmed shrubs that lined the walkways. It wasn't until several years later, when I had gained more "maturity," that I gave in and planted a neat line of colorful zinnias along the sidewalk.

I must be gaining perspective. Now only a small portion of my yard is taken up by grass, and every year that portion shrinks. I'm even considering buying a lawn mower. Where once I compared it to excessive drudgery and responsibility, I now look upon yardwork as "therapy."

A wild assortment of colorful, sweet-smelling flowers now bloom in wild abandon in my yard. They are well taken care of. I carefully shop for flowers that will enjoy the soil composition in my front yard which is different than in my backyard and different than along the sides of my house. If a certain variety of plant finds any of this soil disagreeable to its digestive system, I gladly buy some soil that it likes. I also make special trips to the local greenhouses to shop for the mixture of fertilizers the flowers need to stay hearty and healthy throughout the various seasons. From time to time, I also actually talk to the plants while I'm pruning them! Now a new hobby has emerged. Not only am I interested in how the plants are growing and blooming outwardly, but I am interested in what's going inside their veins as well: I've taken up grafting certain varieties with others.

My daughter thinks I'm gaining perspective, too. Actually, she used the words *getting older*. This name-calling occurred last summer when I took her on a Sunday drive. The sun radiant in the blue sky, we drove along winding roads. I said, "Oh look," pointing in the direction of a house whose yard was adorned with beds of roses, "aren't those beautiful?"

"Yeah," she sighed with no enthusiasm. A few miles down the road she sighed again, "This is so boring. When are we going to *do* something?"

We hadn't gone much further before I said, "Look over there at those lovely flowers!" I pointed toward a field in full bloom.

"They look like weeds to me, Mom." She all but yawned.

"Jen," I said, repeating family history, "you may not appreciate these now, but someday you will."

"Oh, please Mom," she said, rolling her eyes.

After a number of failed attempts at sparking her interest, a novel idea occurred to me, "How about we stop for an ice cream cone?"

Her eyes lit up, and she sat up straighter in her seat, "Yes! That would be great!"

For a brief period my perspective was so my own that I'd forgotten just how I'd evolved to that appreciation. I'd forgotten how, at an earlier time in my life, it was ice cream cones that inspired my true appreciation.

Time and maturity has granted me a deeper appreciation for nature's beauty, and for understanding that you can't force either flowers or children to grow before their time.

Though I didn't bring it to her attention, during the last few months my daughter still lived at home, she took to buying potted plants for her room. Now that she is out on her own, she periodically orders freshly cut flowers from the greenhouse.

In light of these developments, I'm saving her a few carefully selected pieces of heirloom pottery my mother gave me when she noticed my thumb had turned green, at a time when "putting down roots" meant more to me than just staying in the same place for a while.

Events do seem to repeat themselves. Mark Twain called it the law of periodical repetition—everything which has happened once must happen again and again and again, in its own time, in its own way.

So is it just a matter of perspective, part of a life cycle that in our youth we seem to overlook and even take for granted the simple, yet spectacular wonders and beauty of nature? The well-known saying, "Stop and smell the roses," suggests it's the pace of life that is the culprit. But is it truly a cycle that occurs in each of us in its own time and in its own way? Just what unseen power can be found in the passage of time that arouses our senses to wake up and appreciate what has always been within our reach and within our view? Will it be for my daughter as it was for me, and as it was for my mother? Is it just a matter of time—and maturity—before she'll be looking for a home with a yard?

And gardening to her heart's content?

20

 Just
Lucky

Far and away the best prize that life offers is the
chance to work hard at work worth doing.

—Theodore Roosevelt

"I'm embarrassed to admit it, but there were times when I didn't even like my son!" the mother told me. "It's difficult to believe that a mother can feel this way, but with Kevin I did. There were times when he just drove me crazy."

"Just what was it that made him so unlikable?" I asked.

"Well, for starters," she answered, rolling her eyes, "he just wasn't very motivated." She held up her hands and began counting off on her fingers, "He didn't like school, he had few if any friends, he didn't like his teachers, he wasn't interested in any extracurricular activities, and unlike his older brother, he wasn't all that excited about sports, either. In fact, though he finally went out for soccer—we had to coerce him into it—often the coach would just 'forget' to call when he wasn't at practice." She shook her head and added knowingly, "I think it was a relief for him when Kevin wasn't there.

"He was a handful at home, too. He frequently fought with his brother and sister. Homework was always a struggle. I had to resort to scare tactics to make him get up in the morning, get dressed and come to the breakfast table on time. Always on restriction, he'd be onto another restriction before he worked off the former one!

"Luckily, it's different now."

Kevin *is* different now. He was a senior when I met him. I'm always interested in young people and often ask a young person *what* brings meaning and motivation to his or her life, what their *plans* are for turning a wish list into accomplished goals, what each sees as being the *purpose* of his or her life, and when each first discovered that purpose. I also want to know if the young person remembers experiencing an "attitudinal change"—a paradigm shift— as a result. Kevin's story is a good representation of what I learned.

"My mother was driving me to soccer practice. I was in the eighth grade at the time. We came to a stop sign and I looked out the window and saw a large cat lying near a park bench licking her wounds. She looked really hurt. I begged mom to let me go over to get a closer look.

"Well, the cat was badly injured, so I coaxed my mother into letting us take it to a local animal hospital. When we arrived there, the vet took care of the cat then released it to our care. My mother was left with the bill for an animal we didn't own, much less know who he belonged to. But she paid the bill anyway!

"We took the sedated cat home and I carried her into my room and laid her on my bed. By now I could tell that her medication was wearing off. Her breathing was labored. From time to time she picked her head up to see what was going on around her, then after just a few seconds her head dropped back down. And her eyes—they had this glassy look of misery, like she thought she should be afraid of me but didn't have the energy to express it. I knew she was in a whole lot of pain. I stroked her soft silky fur and I talked gently to her, trying as best I could to soothe her. She hardly noticed. Inside, I just felt this pain for her—almost like I felt it *with* her. I wanted to make it go away.

"For some reason, tears came to my eyes. Here I was sitting on my bed, stroking this cat that belonged to someone else and crying. I had never seen the cat before. I didn't understand these feelings. At first I thought maybe the tears were for the cat who was hurt and lying here without her owner's soothing voice. I know that at those times when I've gotten sick at school and found myself lying on the couch in the nurse's office, the one place I'd always rather be is home in my own bed. Just knowing that my mother is somewhere in the house is comforting.

"Then, I thought that maybe my feelings were about gratitude to my mother because she consented to helping an injured cat. Paying the vet bill was more than she could afford—it was a really expensive thing for her to do. She didn't know who the cat belonged to either. It wasn't like she'd get reimbursed. I felt bad that this had cost her, and since I didn't have a job, I couldn't help her with the bill.

"But then it dawned on me that maybe my feelings were about me. Most of the time I felt bored with everything and everyone around me. I often had this lost, kind of out-of-place feeling inside . . . like I never fit in or had a place I felt comfortable. I was always getting in trouble for this or that, and never cared much about anything or felt like what I did mattered, except when I felt these strong feelings that pulled at me every time I found myself helping an animal. It was all at once this reverence, humility and appreciation for wanting to help.

"This made me think about the cat's owner, and I realized that whoever it was would be getting worried about the cat. I went to the garage, got a cardboard box, cut it apart so that I had a large flat surface, and wrote, 'Lost your cat? Call 827-4534.' I took it down to the stop sign and tacked it to the post.

"As I was walking home, the most weird—actually not so *weird* as *interesting*—feelings came over me. I looked down at the sidewalk as I crossed the street and saw this tall mustard plant in full bloom there. For some reason, the sight of it instantly triggered the idea that I wanted to be a veterinarian. Then, like almost instantly, an assortment of feelings rushed into my mind. Immediately, I realized—*I knew for sure*— that I was most happy when I was with animals. But not just in their presence, like when I was horseback riding or at the zoo, but rather, when I was helping them, like all the times I had rescued a wounded or sick dog or cat or bird. Whether they were lost, hurt or simply hungry, I always took them in and helped them on their way. There was this recognition of a lot of feelings, and these feelings took on *meaning*. I realized that what I was doing was important and that what I did made a difference. I felt *honorable* and like I had a greater purpose when I was caring for animals.

"This incident helped me understand, in a big way, what it was that captured my attention most, where I fit and what made me feel most satisfied. I can still visualize the crack in the sidewalk at that moment when I decided that I was going to be a vet. It was very freeing, I wanted to run the rest of the way home! Suddenly, I had the urge to get busy. I wanted to find a newspaper to see if there were any part-time jobs in an animal clinic, or maybe even in a pet store. I began wondering if I was smart enough to be a veterinarian, and if it was too late to get better grades in school in order to get into a college. I found myself wondering how long it would take me to become a vet, even where I would go to school, where I would practice.

"It was such an energizing feeling. All of sudden I felt on track. Life mattered, I had things to do. I was important after all. Dreams flooded my mind and filled my head with visions. I saw myself in college, I saw myself in a small practice with other vets, then in a practice of my own and then in an animal hospital that I had built.

"Well, someone did come for the cat—a guy who lived not more than seven blocks away. It was funny because I had never seen the cat before and I usually walked down that very street on my way to school.

"The man was so grateful. He couldn't afford to repay my mother, though he did promise to trim the trees and hedges in exchange for her paying the vet's bill. I felt good knowing that we'd helped. We'd done the right thing by helping to save an animal's life.

"I still have a soft spot in my heart for that cat—I guess I always will. You know, she comes around to visit now and then. I'll occasionally see her on my way to school. Her name is Lucky. Kind of fits, doesn't it? I think she's grateful. She knows. I think animals know when we help them. I took a psychology course just to get some insight into my idea. I think being a vet will be a very important way to spend my life. I'm a senior now, and I still have my heart set on it!"

After hearing Kevin's story, I later asked his mother if she could chronicle these events as clearly as Kevin could. I asked her, "What do you think Kevin will choose as a career?"

Instantly, she replied, "My son wants to be a vet."

"Has that always been his goal?" I asked.

"Oh yes," she replied, "For as long as I can remember."

"When did Kevin decide to be a vet?" I pressed.

"I don't know, it's been so long."

"No, think about it," I encouraged. "*When* did he make the decision?"

"Really," she said, "I don't remember."

"Was there ever a time when your son *changed?*" I asked. "Was there a time when Kevin went from seemingly one personality to another?"

"Actually, there was," she replied. "There was this *magical time* when Kevin in many ways did change. Out of nowhere, he was *on fire*. The lights just came back on. He began studying, he got along better with his teachers, he was easier to talk with and he seemed interested in so many things. Other kids began wanting to spend time with him and inviting him to go places. It was just the most incredible thing. From *one* day on, it seemed as if Kevin took charge of his life. He had conviction. It was wonderful. I really admire my son. He's a wonderful young man."

"Yes, I'm sure he is," I said. "Did he ever change his mind?"

"No," she replied.

"You mean, he never, ever, wavered?" I asked.

"Oh, sure," she said. "When Kevin was a second semester junior, he didn't know if he wanted to be a *large* animal vet or a *small* animal vet!"

I asked Kevin if he had ever changed his mind about that goal. "Absolutely not. Never!" he replied without hesitation. "I've written so many term papers about it. I work part-time in a pet store, and I've taken the courses I need to prepare for a college that offers a degree in it. No, I'm very sure I'm going to be a vet."

Today, Kevin is a veterinarian. He treats my animals out of his busy office, *Lucky Pet Care Center*. One might attribute his success to what he calls "his purpose," and the genuine affinity and compassion he brings to the care and healing of animals. His work is much more than just a profession, it's also his passion.

"Kevin, why do you think you were able to come to such a clear sense of purpose at such a young age?" I once asked him. With the same grin he flashed as a senior in high school, Kevin replied, "Just Lucky, I guess."

21

Angel Mommy

It's lack of love we die from.

—Margaret Atwood

Sammy knew no one in the center, but despite that, it was a respite from the blows the cherub-faced little girl received at home from the hands of those she loved.

"Okay," the day-school teacher at the center for battered children said, "today we're going to draw a picture of Mommy and Daddy."

A perplexed frown crimped over Sammy's soulful, big round brown eyes. The four-year-old thought it over.

Sammy, named after her father, had never seen her daddy, so she was at a loss drawing him. Tossing her long black curls to one side, she gazed up at the ceiling a moment, crossed her arms, then decided to go on. Mommy, now that was easier to conjure up. The soft features of her tiny round face screwed up in concentration. She put her crayon to her large sheet of paper and drew a picture of an angry woman coming at her with an ominously raised hand.

Upon seeing the frightening picture, a teacher's aide took the child aside. Sitting down next to her, the teacher's aide drew her a "new" picture, one of a woman with kind eyes, a happy smile and arms stretched out wide. With open curiosity and yearning, the tiny-boned and slender little girl studied it momentarily. With great haste, Sammy promptly drew large angel wings on the image before her. The beautiful child then stood back and studied it again. Sammy dropped to her knees, then lay down on the floor. Stretching her arms out as far as they could reach, she embraced the angel.

"Mommy," she said slowly, softly, lovingly. "Mommy . . ."

Angels are said to be the guardians of hope and wonder, the keepers of magic and dreams. It is also said that angels guard and protect children, just as parents should. The lack of protection little Sammy received from her parents didn't diminish her faith in something good though invisible that she equated with love, beauty and nurturing.

"With her background, one has to wonder where this child learned of angels," the childcare worker later said to me.

"Perhaps Sammy just knew it in her heart," I said. Perhaps, she was even taught it by an angel who guarded and protected her tender, young heart, giving it a home when it had nowhere else to go.

I later talked with a psychologist about this episode. "Even in the midst of the most desperate of conditions, the fragile spirit of a child searches for the unconditional love of a parent," Dr. Levine told me.

The road for this young child and her mother, who are now receiving treatment and counseling, will be long and difficult. "It takes a great deal of *time* and *effort* to unlearn what may be a lifetime of wounds passed from one generation to the next, and to heal from them," Dr. Levine said. "It takes *time* and *desire* to relearn how to parent in ways that fulfill a child's need for unconditional love from his or her parents."

Unfortunately, far too many children are painfully surviving, not lovingly thriving throughout the world. As Dr. Levine commented, "Far too many children live in an X-rated world. They have no security blanket to drag behind them. They don't have a room to clean up. They want to be carried. They need to be carried. Their pictures grace no one's dresser."

With my many years of working with families, I knew this to be true. For many children, their nightmares come in the daytime as well as at night. Their monsters are real. In light of this, we need to think of ourselves as parents on a more universal level, to find the heart to give and forgive. We must do so on behalf of those parents who are themselves working through chaos, past pains, selfish and undisciplined caretaking, and whatever fears, prejudices, ignorance or injuries have prevented them from learning to be "angel Mommies."

"Luckily," Dr. Levine said, "For parents who abuse their children, for whatever reason, recovery and forgiveness is possible." Let us hope they seek it. In the meantime, we must remember *our* role. The first step is to fill the void of love and affection in the lives of suffering children—and their parents, as well—with an open heart and open arms. Then, we must provide protection in other ways.

Tonight this little girl and thousands like her are safe because of the dedicated work and funds donated on behalf of children whose "guardians" have yet to learn how to show love and affection in ways that allow little bodies to be protected in safe ways, little souls to be protected in nurturing ways, and little hearts to be protected in loving ways.

May we all search our hearts and share our own "angel Mommy" with those whose angel exists only on paper and with those parents who cannot as yet hold their little ones *safely* in their arms.

22   Supervision 101

Never mistake knowledge for wisdom.
One helps you make a living;
the other helps you make a life.

—Sandra Carey

I was sitting poolside at a friend's condominium home, seething about what to do with two employees whose constant need for supervision was taxing my patience. I silently rehearsed the words to use in our inevitable "come to Jesus" meeting, where I planned to give them both notice and be done with them once and for all. Lost in thought,

I was startled by the squeals of joy and exuberance from a pair of rambunctious children. They ran past me and cannonballed into the other end of the pool. The children—who appeared to be about six and eight years old—frolicked without a care in the invigorating water, not far from the posted sign "Parents Are Responsible for the Supervision of Their Children."

Several minutes later, a young woman with a freshly diapered toddler on her hip appeared, tossed hellos to those who greeted her, and scanned the clusters of people poolside and those in the water. With a fixed glare in the direction of the two children, she briskly walked to the side of the pool. Instantly, her children knew they had disobeyed her. They scurried out of the water. One look into their mother's squinting brown eyes conveyed the status of their predicament. The children surveyed the sunbathers nearby and quickly factored in their advantage of being in the midst of other people. Surely this would momentarily buffer their plight of being disciplined. They tried using it to their advantage. Dripping water and blank-eyed innocence, they shamelessly (and loudly) inquired, *"What,* Mom?"

Kids can be so articulate and aware.

Unruffled, yet firm, she said, "I told you to wait for me, that you could not go in the pool without me. I'm afraid you won't be allowed to go in the pool anymore today. Dry off and change." Said with an air of calm authority, this netted immediate results: bug-eyed indignation, a flicker of mutiny and trembling lips from her eight-year-old daughter. Her six-year-old son got only as far as mutiny, a shame, because most mothers waver on the length of restriction when faced with trembling lips. Belligerently, the boy scowled and screamed the words that doomed them: "That's not fair!"

The mother's cheeks flushed. She looked up at her growing audience of onlookers and rubbed the baby's back vigorously to still a telltale tremor of embarrassment. Sheepishly she said, "If I had a dime for every time the lad uttered those words, I could give Bill Gates some serious competition!" By this time the eight-year-old's trembling lips had escalated to tears, then sobs, then wails.

Having once been in her shoes, I knew she probably wanted to join in, but motherhood offers few, if any, time-outs. Instead, she mustered up the energy reserved for the unpleasant but necessary task of assigning consequences to her children's incorrigible behavior. In preparation, she drew a long deep sigh. Then, in a voice that would have made John Wayne proud, she declared, "A mom's got to do what a mom's got to do!" Now resolute, a pillar of guidance, she looked at both children and calmly and authoritatively said, "Back to the house, now!"

Sure that it was their mother—and not the children—who were in charge here, the children picked up their towels and headed sullenly, yet obediently, toward the pool gate.

With a last sweeping glance around the pool she sweetly said, "Sorry for the commotion! My *darlings* and I are going home now."

"I'm impressed!" I said as she passed. "Your kids didn't put up much of a fight. I guess they know better! I could sure use your supervisory style to straighten out a couple of my employees! The only difference between your children and the two of them is that you only had to tell them once."

"Thanks," she said, laughing. Perhaps feeling that it would be okay to allow her children some cooling down time, she paused for a moment and we began to talk.

"It sounds like we have similar jobs!" she said. "The only difference is that you can fire your employees, and I can't fire my children, although some days I would like to!" Her eyes twinkled as she tossed her head back and laughed wholeheartedly. Then in a soft and loving voice, she remarked, "It's a lot of work but I'm in it for the long haul with these children." Once again her good humor took over and she said with a wide smile, "Though there are days when going to work in an office would be a vacation compared to juggling the constant needs of three children!"

"You may be more successful with your children than I am with the two 'children' in my office," I said, wryly.

With a thoughtful look, she said, "From the sound of it, neither one of our jobs is for the faint of heart." She paused and, chuckling, said, "They *were* pretty good about it today, but I'm not always so successful." Once again, she laughed freely and happily, and then added, "At least it's never dull. The hard part is being consistent, and sometimes having to be the bad guy. Like now. Quite honestly I was looking forward to swimming in the pool with them, but it's more important they learn boundaries and consequences for acting outside of integrity. I guess that means pay now, and play later!" Brown eyes sparkling, she said tenderly, "It's a good thing I love them so much."

"Well, I admire you," I said sincerely. "You're a wonderful role model. Your children are fortunate to have someone who not only understands what it takes to guide them, but follows through on their learning the lessons you're teaching."

"Oh, thanks," she said. "I don't know about the wonderful role model bit. I serve my share of cold cereal. I'm sure my kids don't know the difference between granola and shinola. But I do know that if they are to learn to be responsible, capable and, most especially, to pull their weight as members of a family, I'll have to do a good job in my role of leading them."

This woman was sharp. I was hoping she would spend a minute more. "You've really thought about this," I said. "You take your parenting skills very seriously. It's commendable!"

"I'm getting it down," she said, once again laughing. "Three young children will teach you quite a bit. It didn't take long to learn the difference between being efficient and being effective, between parenthood and parenting, between teaching my children clever behavior and teaching them responsible behavior."

"So, where did you get your degree in managing human behavior?" I asked. "Or were you always so proficient?"

"Oh, no," she asserted. "At first I felt really inadequate. I had these niggling doubts that constantly churned beneath the surface. 'Am I too hard on them? . . . or too easy?' Then I thought, what business do I have raising children without a degree in child psychology? What would Drs. Spock, Brazelton, Dobson or Leach advise?' As I got into the job, I realized I would be better served by a degree in supervision! But I didn't have one, so I applied common sense instead."

"Eight years of rearing children must surely be equivalent to a Ph.D.!" I said.

"That's for sure," she said, emphatically. "For sure it's a practicum in Supervision 101!" She paused for a moment and then thoughtfully said, "You know, it's more like Mother Skills 101. It's really a matter of understanding human behavior, isn't it? Mine as much as theirs. That my children learn to be responsible, caring and law-abiding citizens is as much a function of my leadership as an outcome of their feelings."

My mind conjured up the image of the two difficult employees.

This had turned out to be quite a conversation, and quite different than my expectations when I acknowledged her less than five minutes earlier for her momentary handling of the situation. "You've learned quite a lot," I said.

Laughing, she said, "You mean I don't need anyone else to reassure me that motherhood and guilt go hand in hand!"

"You don't look or sound like you spend too much time on guilt," I said. "So with a degree in mother-skill experience, what philosophy have you formulated?"

Without hesitation she chanted, *"Human beings prefer doing things in their own way, in their own time and, given an option, will sometimes do as they please."*

"That's funny!" I said, laughing.

"But true," she countered. "So I realized my job was not just a matter of disciplining my children, but more a job of teaching my children how to lead themselves; of helping each child set his own course and providing a personal compass to get there. This means I'd better be clear on how

I help them head in the direction they should be heading."

"What do you mean . . . a personal compass?" I asked, wanting to explore her analogy.

Explaining, she said, "COMPASS is an acronym I use with my kids. It stands for: Control, Order, Motivation, Planning, Ask, Sharing, and Synergy. It's an easy way to remember the different elements needed to go in the direction we as a family want to go in. Together we talk about the rules and boundaries, and consequences for not following them. I want my children to take responsibility for their behavior, but I'm the boss! I decide if they're staying within the boundaries appropriately. My role is to do this fairly and consistently so they know they can count on the feedback." Making a scowl, she added in fun, "And swift! Knowing this leaves them free from guessing and game playing. This doesn't mean they don't test the rules periodically, however! As you can see, they did today! But, they're pretty good, they're learning. Overall, I'm very pleased with their understanding and the way they follow my direction."

"I can hardly wait to learn what C means," I said, eager to understand her analogy.

"It sounds complicated, but it's not. My kids are bright and I have high expectations for them. So, to answer your question, C is for control—of ourselves; it's a personal code of conduct. O is for order. This is about respecting the basic needs of the others we live with and is necessary to prioritize what we want to do and the time we have to do it. M is for motivation—taking care of oneself so you feel energized to get your work done. You know, it's about the importance of exercise, eating right, getting enough sleep, stuff like that.

P is for planning—setting goals and objectives. This is designing the map that shows us what we want to accomplish. *A* is for asking for help or advice. *S* is for sharing. And the last *S* is for synergy—the importance of being a family, a team of people who love and care about each other and each other's needs. I deal with all this on their level, but the principles are the same at any age, aren't they?"

"Yes, they are," I said, my mind once again on my two employees.

"Simply put," she said, "the components of COMPASS are the building blocks for getting my children to stand on their own two feet—to take responsibility for themselves in all things. It's my role to be the leader. My job is to teach it, teach it and teach it again, until they get it. They're good kids. When they don't follow the rules, I assume I may not be teaching it right, that is, I haven't yet found the way to impress the importance of it upon them. It's just a matter of time and my willingness to help them want that for themselves as well."

I was amazed. Not only at the level of this stimulating conversation, but by her viewpoint. She believed that even young children could learn the step-by-step process of self-management.

I thought about how I saw my employees. I saw them as two irresponsible problems and was treating them as such. Was my paradigm of them as much a part of the problem as their refusal to take the baton of responsibility? I tried to reframe it in my mind. I had recruited vibrant, high-achieving, success-oriented people. Where had I missed the boat with these two young employees? What had gone wrong? They were capable and bright. Why wouldn't they pull their weight in making a mature and positive contribution to the company?

I thought about what the young mother said and how truly similar our jobs were. Whether raising children or supervising employees, we're all deeply involved in the art of inspiring others by applying correct principles of leadership. I thought about my concerns. They centered around wanting my staff to be as passionate about the goals of the company as I was; to turn in a peak performance, giving their best zestfully, not grudgingly. I wanted them to act conscientiously and ethically and to adhere to a code of conduct that was by any measure a high standard. On a personal level I encouraged my grown daughter to take responsibility for her life, to recognize that she is the instrument of her own performance. Why not use a similar strategy with my staff? Why not apply Mother Skills 101?

"What part of your compass do you find the most challenging?" I asked her.

"Probably motivation. Sometimes making the connection between work and sacrifice now for some reward in the future is tough, especially on the little day-to-day stuff," she said. "And if I use the wrong incentives to motivate my children, I know that I'm spending energy in a way that only creates within them a misaligned ability to do what it takes to garner the carrots. And that's not what I want. I want my children skilled at making sound decisions for themselves and to think about how these affect others around them."

I knew she was right. My task was to help my two employees create for themselves a desire to produce, achieve, excel. Only then would there be an advance in their performance that produced an increase in profit, growth and positive change.

"Well, I better run," she said, glancing at her watch. "My children have had enough time to think, and we need to talk things through."

I thought about the talk I was also about to have back at my office, and smiled to myself at our similar positions. "If you're ever looking for a job," I said handing her my card, "call me. I could use such finely honed skills in my office."

"Well," she said once again laughing. "If this doesn't go well, I just might take you up on that offer!"

I reflected on the analogy of the compass, and how refreshing and simple the young mother had made such an important lesson for her children. What a wonderful gift to give her children: the tools to determine their own destiny and purpose; to choose to be useful, responsible, honorable, compassionate; to matter; to stand for something, and to make a difference in the world around them.

Perhaps the application of *mother skills* are as useful as those taught in Supervision 101.

Life Leaps

Love is the river of life in this world.

—Henry Ward Beecher

The early morning two-mile run with my two dogs was by now a daily ritual. This began at the house and stopped midway at the mouth of the lagoon. My two dogs looked forward to cooling off in the current and playing fetch-the-stick-in-the-water before their vigorous run home.

Samson, the four-year-old yellow lab, and Sadie, my two-year-old basset hound, loved this time of exercise and anxiously looked forward to it. Each morning, they half-heartedly played in the yard, never venturing very far from the house. Every so often they ran from one glass door to the other searching eagerly to catch a glimpse of me heading to the garage, hoping that I was on my way to get their harnesses.

How different they were. When Sadie saw me head for the garage, her happiness overcame her. Around and around her short little legs carried her, propelled by her busy tail. Samson was no less vigilant. When he saw me lace up my running shoes, he ran to where the collars hung and sat proudly. His beautiful, silky golden-haired body erect and his head up, ready to wear his collar, he thumped his tail expressing a more dignified joy.

Sadie and Samson: roommates, playmates, accomplices. Each knew the intricacies of the other. Each tolerated the other. Each knew the other's limits. Just as children learn exactly how to play their parents, Sadie knew she could bite and pull on Samson's ears and he would take her play and abuse mercilessly. Just as children sense precisely where to draw the line before they are reprimanded, Sadie, too, knew exactly when to back off to save herself from being cuffed by Samson. Instinctively, each deciphered precisely what the different pitches of the other's barks meant. One pitch initiated free-for-all roughhousing. Another meant "Stay out of my bowl or you'll be more sorry than not!" Sometimes it meant "Hey, come look at this!"

Each dog had a distinctly different personality and never was this more apparent than out on our daily run. Each was preoccupied with his or her own instinctual habits. Samson, the observer, the loyal one, kept his eye on me. He wanted to be where I was. Always staying close at hand, he was a protector, a guardian. He also lifted his leg to wet on every patch of anything that smelled as if another animal had crossed its path. It was his way of saying, "*I've* been here!"

For Sadie it was a total loss of time and place. Nostrils aimed downward, she was goaded on by whatever she smelled. Yes, Sadie was a different matter. She would bound off, her elongated white- black- and brown-speckled body at a full swaggering run. Her oversized ears—one black, one brown—flopped as they dragged along. Her nose to the ground the entire way, she sniffed ceaselessly for anything that possessed a scent. Any attempts I might make to call her back on course were viewed as a distraction. "Sadie, get back here!" I'd yell. She'd grudgingly glance up at me with drooping jowls and drooping eyes that pleaded not to be deprived in this way. Then she'd quickly drop her head and return to her blissful quest. If I didn't keep an eye on her, she was gone. The smell of a rabbit, fox, gopher, ground squirrel—whatever—could take her off in the direction of the hills, where she would disappear until the scent of her object of desire completely eluded her.

Usually this meant she was on her way to being lost, though Sadie never considered it that way. Ever playful, any human—though children at play were her favorite—could make her feel right at home. She would forget her first family and tag along with her newfound friends. I never trusted that she could find her way home.

She never missed her family and home enough to keep from straying: out of sight, out of mind. When she was out

of my sight, it usually meant I had to go searching for her—
or listen to my answering machine to discover who found
a lost dog. Two years old, she would forever be in her "terrible twos."

The halfway point was the lagoon. Sometimes the dogs
arrived before me and jumped in, romping around in the
water. Other times, like today, they sat at the water's edge
and waited for me. As I did nearly every day, I picked up a
piece of broken branch and flung it high into the air above
the water. Taking note of the clean-smelling ions, I looked
forward to the joy of watching my two pets play in the
water once again. Unlike yesterday, the day before and the
day before that, neither dog jumped in the water. Today
both stood by the water's edge, reluctant to jump in. For a
moment, I had the fleeting sense that there was something
not quite the same today. The water seemed particularly
dark. Its gushing sounds were somehow tense; its movements too rapid. I brushed this intuition aside, preferring
instead to treat it as a passing notion.

"Go for it, Samson!" I called to the big dog, who was the
leader of the two. Excited about playing, Samson bounded
in the direction my hand pointed. Once he saw the stick sail
out over the water, however, he stopped abruptly. Sadie
just watched.

"What deadheads!" I teased, certain they were acting on
some whim of laziness. "You guys are no fun today. I've
never seen you like this. That run didn't tire you out this
much! C'mon, let's play." They looked at me. Tongues
panting and tails wagging, they ran to me, colliding as they
clamored to get their ears rubbed and heads petted.

"Why aren't you guys playing in the water?" I cajoled playfully. "I can't stay all day. I have to get back to the office."

Certainly more encouragement was called for. I wrapped my arms around my spotted basset's plump, little white belly, carried her to the water's edge, and tossed her in as I had done before on several occasions.

"Okay, Samson," I said playfully to the yellow lab. "What'll it be? Are you going in or are you waiting for me to toss you in, too?" I bounded over to him, but just as I was about to hoist him in I caught sight of my basset—floundering in the dangerous current.

Her eyes cast about wildly in fear as she labored to get to shore. In the same instant, I saw a small log sail swiftly by in the water, then disappear with sudden violence beneath the water's surface, sucked in by a powerful downward swirling vortex. Immediately my eyes darted to my basset, who at that instant was swallowed by the water's swirling force.

"Sadie!" I shouted. I watched her body bob up and down, surfacing one moment only to be forcefully pulled under the water the next by the mighty current brutally gushing downstream in the direction of the ocean. I ran along the shore line, trying to find a place that looked safe enough for me to jump in and save her.

"Sadie!" I yelled again, trying to reassure my pet that my help was coming. I searched desperately for a place where the water didn't look as menacing so I could rush in and rescue her. My instincts kept shouting back at me, "No, not here, it's too dangerous. No, not here either . . . or here." Panic set in. My little dog was in trouble—more than she could handle—and I was too scared to help. Trying to find a solution, my mind raced through the options.

His courage greater than mine, Samson knew precisely what was needed. Valiantly leaping into the mysterious waters, he furiously paddled against its mighty force to reach his playmate. Drenched, his coat lay slick against his body, making the muscles on his back and the sleek tendons of his shoulders visible. They alternately bulged then contracted in strenuous effort. He held his head up out of the water, his brown eyes glinting with determination as they focused on Sadie.

Struggling against the water's unpredictable fury, Samson finally reached his companion. Then he did a most loving, amazing and brave feat. With a surge of power he dove beneath the water and underneath her, then lunged forcefully upward, like a dolphin jumping for a treat after a performance in a water show. He had given himself as her life raft.

Still wild-eyed, Sadie battled not just to survive her fear and the savage force of the water, but also to stay on Samson's back. His slippery coat more a slide than a raft, Sadie struggled to stay in place. Her short legs paddled as she tried desperately to cling to him. His long ones paddled to reach shore. One second she slid one way, then recklessly clawed her way to the top of his back again before sliding the other and pulling her way back again. All Sadie's might centered on staying on top of Samson as they made the arduous journey to the water's edge.

Once he'd slugged his way to shore, Samson dumped his playmate on the bank and tenderly licked her disoriented face. Exhausted, Sadie weakly returned a few of Samson's licks, deferring to his caretaking. Then she stood on legs that were momentarily wobbly and shook herself off. She leaned into Samson's nudges and licks as if grateful for his bringing her to safety, grateful for his presence in her life. Samson continued licking her as if he, too, were grateful for her safety and grateful for her presence—even if she was a nuisance. Filled with gratitude and relief myself, I drank in the sight of them together. I was curious about the words they might have expressed if English had been their language.

Not that words could have expressed more than their actions did.

"Oh, Samson," I pleaded, still shaking with fright while leaping over patches of tall wild grass and hopping through puddles of mud to get to them. Wanting to praise him, I reached out my hand and called him by name to come to me for adulation. Obviously miffed, his eyes met mine. He furiously shook his drenched coat as if he *wanted* the large drops of water to splash all over me.

Reflecting on how I'd ignored my pets' instinctive caution earlier, I did feel bad. At the same time, I was thankful for Samson's heroics, atoning for my error in judgment. I wondered how I missed it.

Replaying the mental vision of Samson's determined leap into the rushing water caused me to think about the times symbolic leaps into dangerous water were made in the lives of people I know and love. I recalled the harrowing experience of my dear friend Jean, the mother of a lovely 19-year-old daughter, Leigh, who had been lured into a circle of friends that encouraged drug use and abuse. Jean suspected that Leigh was addicted and way beyond making healthy choices for herself. Jean knew she would do whatever she could to help her daughter choose to live drug-free.

One night her heart told her, in no uncertain terms, she must reach out to Leigh. Instinctively, she knew her daughter was in need of rescuing. Filled with anxiety and not knowing what she was walking into, this determined mother went to where her daughter was staying and found her in the midst of eight of her newfound friends, all "high as a kite." Looking around the room, it was apparent that this was not just a case of a few college kids partying together. Immediately, she knew her daughter was in grave danger and needed medical as well as psychological care.

Though calm on the outside, she was terrified. Here were young adults who looked downright dangerous. Here was her beloved daughter, once an honor student and star athlete, now looking sad and lifeless. Like the others, Leigh had a bandanna wrapped around her head and ink drawings on her hands and up her arms. Knowing that her daughter was too old to force, she calmly but firmly announced that she was staying until Leigh decided to come with her. Though the standoff between mother and daughter lasted half the night, it ended with the two of them leaving together. They returned the following day to collect her things. With loving assistance, Jean guided her daughter back to a productive and healthy life.

Leigh credits her mother with saving her life.

There are those times in our lives when our instincts of self-preservation—those sensory instincts that warn us of danger—are overcome by greater instincts that function on a deeper level: the level of the heart. Guided by love, those powers allow us to act with undaunted courage and unwavering loyalty. As did Jean. And Samson.

24 That Space Called Loneliness

Love is the emotional flow of
energy that nourishes, extends and preserves.
Its eternal goal is life.

—Smiley Blanton

In a more or less troubled tone, my friend Julianne said to me, "I've been so lonely recently, but I just can't seem to place it. Everything in my life is going well, I have no complaints. Still, I just feel so homesick; for what, I don't know. It's an elusive longing, a vague empty feeling, like a cloud over an otherwise perfect day."

Julianne was normally upbeat and positive. I knew these nebulous feelings greatly concerned her or else she wouldn't have brought them up. "Maybe you should take some time off," I suggested. "Visit your parents, especially if you're homesick. I remember you mentioning that you haven't seen them in well over a year . . ."

Before I could finish, she said, "I *do* need to connect with my parents, but this is actually a much *deeper* loneliness. It's different from the empty-nest syndrome I went through when my children left for college. It's unlike the sense of emptiness I experienced when my grown children moved to other cities and began lives of their own. It's different than the sense of loss I felt when my husband and I divorced. It's all *very* different. As strange as this sounds, I'm homesick for what I *know*: I feel as though I'm *misplaced*, that I'm supposed to be somewhere else. It's like there's an inner beeper going off, beckoning me, but for *what* or *where*, I don't know or understand."

I thought about Julianne's "unspecific" pining as I sat among 247 impatient passengers. We were shoulder-to-shoulder inside the hot, stuffy cabin of a stationary jumbo jet waiting for our transatlantic flight. I had been aboard the plane for more than an hour; it was held captive by daunting winds and sheets of water pounding down from the blackened clouds above. The spirits of the passengers lifted as the plane pulled away from the gate, then were dashed when it joined what looked like a parade of lights. Numerous other jets were lined up awaiting the mandatory go-ahead from the control tower.

Another empty 90 minutes passed as we inched along.

"What a way to begin a 12-hour flight," grumbled one frustrated businessman seated across the aisle from me. "At this rate we'd get there faster if we broke out the life boats and started paddling." Several surrounding passengers chuckled in agreement just as the voice of the captain crackled over the intercom. He announced that it was time to prepare for takeoff. Half-hearted cheers and applause came from several of the passengers as the flight attendants walked down the aisles inspecting for fastened seat belts, trays in the upright position, and carry-on baggage properly stowed overhead or under seats.

The passengers may not have cheered if they knew what a turbulent ride lay ahead. Even the sure-footed flight attendants stumbled at the rigorous bumps and drops of the plane. The pilots searched different altitudes for smoother air. Dinner was postponed. During a particularly forceful bounce in the air, the businessman who was ready to paddle his way across the Atlantic unexpectedly found a surprised and embarrassed flight attendant in his lap. It would have been a more humorous moment if the storm we were flying through was not so ominous. I had made this transatlantic flight many times and always thought of myself as a seasoned traveler, but this violent jostling was the worst I'd ever encountered. I knew the easiest way to make this trip was to sleep as much as possible. Though odds were against it, I did the best I could with the undersized blanket and pillows allotted.

Several hours later I awakened to a friendly attendant offering the dinner that had been shaken beyond recognition. I was relieved to see we had found calmer skies.

The woman in the seat next to me sighed heavily and said, "What a flight, huh? I was really looking forward to this trip, but it sure has been a nerve-wracking seven hours!"

"That's for sure," I agreed.

"I'm hoping the rest of the way isn't more of the same," she said. Animated and obviously excited, she added, "I'm going home to visit my family. I haven't seen them in four years. I'm so looking forward to it!"

"I'll bet they're really looking forward to seeing you, too," I said, thinking how difficult I would find not seeing my family for that long a time. My thoughts returned to Julianne who hadn't seen her parents in over a year. I genuinely liked Julianne. I also empathized with her feelings . . . and found her longings familiar.

"Where do they live?" I asked my fellow traveler.

"My parents reside in London proper. They just bought a huge old house built in the 1800s."

As she said these words, thoughts of my Great-Auntie's house came to mind. I had grown up in the house next to it and visited my Great-Auntie nearly every day. Great-Auntie's house was a grand, old three-story house with 15 rooms. Folklore had it that somewhere in its walls a treasure was buried. Every generation of the family clan who lived in the house was said to have felt its presence, though it was so well-hidden no one had ever found it. It cast a wonderful enchantment over the house. Somewhere in the depths of the heart of this magnificent wooden temple, a secret was hiding. I wondered if, like my Great-Auntie's house, the human temple harbored a secret deep within, casting a yearning sense of being misplaced over our nature—as Julianne was so aptly feeling. In *The Wizard of Oz*, the Scarecrow wanted brains or wisdom. The Lion wanted courage, and the Tin Man wanted a heart or love. Dorothy was homesick; she just wanted to go home where she knew she'd find all those things.

Perhaps like Dorothy—and Julianne—we are all scripted to be homesick. Homesick for what we *know*. To be where we know we will find *all things*.

Time passed and I recognized the change of flight angle as an indication we were approaching our destination. Once again the confident voice of the captain rang throughout the cabin explaining that we had been able to outrun the storm and had made up a substantial amount of time due to strong tail winds. Then he paused and continued. "However, I've got good news and bad news . . ."

"Oh no, here it comes, let's hear the bad news first," moaned the woman beside me. As if complying with her request, the captain proceeded, "Let's start with the bad news. I've just received word that our destination airport is reporting a very dense fog layer." Believing the implication must mean another lengthy delay to this already grueling trip, moans and groans were heard from passengers taxed beyond their normal limits of endurance. Again anticipating the probable response to his bad news, the captain quickly added, "Now the good news. As you know our destination airport is a major air hub for continental Europe and is often fogged in. Fortunately, it's equipped with the world's most up-to-date electronic instrument guided-landing system. This means that planes equipped with advanced avionics, such as ours, can be landed there in virtually zero-zero conditions. In other words, we can land with no ceiling and with an RVR (Runway Visibility Range) down below 300 feet." A cautious hope trickled throughout the cabin, as the captain continued to reassure us. "This Instrument Landing System, ILS for short, can just about land the plane itself," he said. "We lock onto the ground base homing signal, and our three onboard auto-pilot computers pretty much do the rest. So in a nutshell, the good news is . . . we're going to go straight in." It seemed that 247 passengers all sighed with relief in unison, and then giggled or at least smiled at the spontaneous, yet perfectly orchestrated chorus of exhales. It was a welcome moment of comic relief.

I sat up in my seat and looked out the window to see the thin gray light of early dawn. *Dense fog?* I thought to myself, *I can't see a thing, this stuff is as thick as pea soup!* I heard the telltale whine and then thump of the landing gear being let down and the slight change in pitch of the engine upon final approach. A nervous feeling sat in the pit of my stomach as I braced myself for what I anticipated to be a landing in keeping with the rest of the trip—rough.

I felt the wheels ever so gently brush the runway upon touchdown, then firmly bite into the tarmac as the reverse thrusters roared. The plane braked evenly as we coasted slowly to the gate. It was a very smooth landing. I collected my carry-on bag and made my way to the front of the plane to exit with the rest of the passengers.

As I approached the flight attendant bidding each trav-eler farewell at the door, the captain exited the cockpit. "Nice landing," I said as he pulled on his jacket.

"Thanks, but that's what really landed the plane, the ILS computer," he replied, pointing toward the myriad of colorful blinking lights from sophisticated instrumentation panels and displays of the cockpit. Astonished, I asked, "Could you see anything?"

"Not outside the cockpit," he said. "We were still up in the soup when the rear wheels touched down, but we were closely monitoring the landing beacon computer display. It shows our position, proper flight path and exactly where the center of the runway is. Auto-pilot flies the plane right down the thing."

"Amazing," I said, and shook my head in wonder as I hurried down the jetway toward passport control and baggage claim.

In avionics the word *integrity* is used to describe a pilot's ability to rely on the accuracy of his instruments and equipment. My apprehensions about landing were clearly not shared by the captain. He, in contrast, trusted the integrity of the ILS system and the accuracy of his onboard computers. I wondered if people—like the jumbo jet— have an innate homing beacon, an inner voice that acts as a signal that we may be off course in reaching our destination. Could the internal pangs of loneliness, homesickness or feelings of disconnection be a clue that we have drifted to a place in our lives where we are no longer aligned with the perfect harmony of abundance that is rightly ours?

Perhaps, like my Great-Auntie's house, the human temple *does* harbor a secret treasure deep within its heart. Perhaps that treasure wants—silently screams—to be found, so it sends a code of longing. This low but constant echo leads us to a majestic map that shows the way to the treasure, our own promised destiny. Is this code so fail-proof that when we try to ignore it by distracting ourselves through alcohol, drugs, work, even service to others, life becomes shrouded in boredom, feelings of worthlessness or worse, grandiose detachment from ourselves, causing an even greater sense of yearning? As Julianne said, "Even though everything in my life is going well—my family is healthy, my work offers challenge and rewards—these things don't buffer the feelings that *something* is missing."

Perhaps we give misguided direction to those in search of the origin of their longing when we encourage them to escape loneliness by entertaining themselves or by "getting involved." When we exhaust ourselves through busy service to others, the voice of loneliness can still haunt us. As theologian Henri Nouwen writes, "The Christian way of life does not take away our loneliness; it protects and cherishes it as a precious gift." Could it be that loneliness is inevitable, inspired by our need to reclaim our spiritual truths?

Months later, Julianne said to me, "Maybe God wasn't serious when he gave us 'free will.' My heart nagged me endlessly. But, for me, the answer wasn't about increased activity, more time with family and friends, or exercise to enhance my well-being via revving up my endorphins. Rather, it was about seeking the presence of God within. When my relationship with God deepened, I became more satisfied in all areas of my life. This in turn deepened my relationship with others, and has renewed my sense of purpose. In a very real sense, my loneliness was a gift that beckoned me to probe for a deeper meaning in life, *my* life."

The notion that we each have an innate beacon, a perfect navigational signal, offers comfort: God is *actively* involved in our lives. Unless we think our lives and that of a mushroom follow a similar destiny, seeking out the origin of this mysterious longing and following it—each in our own way—may just be the most important mission of our hearts.

25	7 x \$486

A single night of universal love could save everything.

—Roland Giguére

One Sunday I noticed a small wet spot near the altar in our church. The next Sunday the spot was a bit bigger. Each Sunday thereafter the spot grew bigger and bigger, until finally, on one particularly wet Sunday, a small pail sat collecting the occasional drip from the ceiling above. The roof was leaking.

It wasn't long before resolving this problem appeared in the form of a memo to our board.

"How can we possibly go back to the congregation and ask for more?" asked Dave, one of seven of us who had volunteered to serve together as the acting board of trustees for our church. "They have given so much already!"

His question was legitimate. It presented a dilemma.

We were responsible for organizing the community service projects and raising funds for the many humanitarian needs of families in and out of our small congregation. As a group dedicated to reaching out and making a difference, the year had been a great success.

"We've asked the congregation for so much already," Margo pointed out. "Just think about it: with projects ranging from supporting an orphanage in Mexico, to sending nine needy teens to church summer camp . . ."

"To providing food and shelter for 18 families in crisis, all in this year," chimed in Robert. "You remember how we asked that our members dig deeper, and then, still $1,200 short, we asked again for one 'final' offering?"

We did. The congregation had rallied time and time again with their enthusiastic support and donations of both time and money. The number of lives we were able to touch and improve was gratifying and worthwhile—all made possible by the selfless sacrifices of this small congregation.

Yet here we sat with *another* need for funds. This time, a contractor's estimate specified we needed to replace exactly $3,402 of a new section of roof for our own church building.

"We can't do it this season, that's all there is to it," Henry said. "We're going to have to put it off until next spring. Unless we can contract a roofing company that won't mind waiting for payment until spring, it's just not going to happen."

"That's risky," Helen said, shaking her head. "We can all see that the damage created by this leak is getting more extensive, and it can only get worse. Like Henry and Robert and Dave, I don't think it's right that we ask this little congregation to foot the bill, but, really, what other choice do we have?"

The prospect of asking the church family to contribute yet more was something none of us were comfortable with, especially when we knew it would be a true hardship for some. Glancing around the room, I looked over each member of the board. We were all successful professionals who had contributed generously throughout the year. Still, as I listened to each of my fellow board members and pondered the situation, I couldn't help but come back to one possible solution.

"What if we looked for the answer here, with us?" I asked.

"How do you mean?" a member of the group asked.

"The only way I think we can all agree to ask our members to give more is if we as their leaders are willing to give more. What if each of us—right now, at this moment— write out a check or make a pledge for whatever we can individually and comfortably afford?" Even though I didn't say so, I knew that with an average of $486 per board member, we'd have the $3,402 we needed.

"Now there's an idea," Helen agreed.

They were all quiet for a moment. Then they looked to each other with hopeful nods and murmurs of approval. The mood in the room lifted from perplexed to pleased.

The room then fell silent as each of us carefully considered how much we were able to give. Though this only took a few minutes, time seemed somehow suspended as we became a study of absorbed concentration. Julia gazed off at the center of the room while chewing on the ends of her glasses. From time to time, Henry, with his brow furrowed, cleared his throat. Running his hand through his thick hair, Robert bit his lip while he deliberated his total. Dave took out his portable cell phone and called his wife. He could be heard in hushed conversation, discussing the amount their family was comfortable donating. Heads cocked, eyes glazed with thought, each member finally, decisively, put their pens to their checkbooks—or a piece of paper representing their contribution—for the amount they were able to give.

"Are we all ready?" Henry inquired once everyone had put down their pens. After our chorused affirmatives, he went to the front of the room to tally the contributions on the board. We all watched with rapt interest as he wrote the amounts of each anonymous donor. When our total was calculated, we found the problem of the leaky roof was solved. Nearly $5,000 had been raised, including one check for the entire amount of $3,402! I looked around the table at the dawning smiles and nodding heads of the other members. Inspired by our respect and appreciation, we all joined in a round of spontaneous applause for each other.

Feeling my own sense of satisfaction, I looked around at the satisfied smiles of the other board members and realized that often solutions to problems are comfortable as well as practical—especially when we respond to the solutions voiced by our hearts.

Big Feet, Little Feet

Love is indescribable and unconditional.
I could tell you a thousand things that it is not,
but not one that it is.

—Duke Ellington

Laurie always set her shoes beside her daddy's shoes. Maybe it was because he was so persistent and patient in teaching her to stand, to put one foot in front of the other, over and over again, all the while holding her by her frail little waist and hips.

Who knows?

Maybe it was because he gently lifted up her little foot and placed it firmly on the tiny bicycle pedal and then alternated it with the same procedure on the other foot and pedal until, at last, the child, foot and pedal cooperated spontaneously and moved rhythmically ahead.

Who knows?

Maybe it was the first solo ride he encouraged by forcing her up the lane path with, "Okay, if you fall down, get up. Come on, let's do it again. You can do it! There, you made it up the path all by yourself! See, I knew you could!"

Who knows?

Her intellectual and physical challenges were so great that others said the time spent developing them wasn't worth it. He didn't see it that way. Her body and mind weren't quite as large as his, but her loving heart and spirit were and, in so being, enlarged her daddy's heart and spirit.

Maybe the persistent, determined and loving man who taught her so many things with her little feet is the reason why every night she places her little shoes beside his size 11Ds.

Isn't this what life is about: one heart enlarging the capacity of another? Big feet guiding little feet, healthy brilliant minds assisting the slower.

This is love and talent used properly.

And why little shoes *want* to rest beside big shoes.

27 Of Eagles . . . and Body Blows

*Square your shoulders to the world, be
not the kind to quit. It's not the load that breaks
you down, it's the way you carry it.*

—Source Unknown

I was recently in Denver presenting a seminar entitled, "Personal Challenge—a Catalyst for Growth and Change." One of the goals was to get participants to think about how a challenge they faced had created change in their lives— for the better. I started the workshop by telling the moving story in David McNally's beautiful book, *Even Eagles Need a Push,* in which the mother eagle gently coaxes her off-spring toward the edge of the nest so they can get on with the business of being an eagle. As is the tradition of the species, eagles build their nests high on the shelf of a sheer rock face. Knowing that below there was nothing but air to support the wings of each "child," the mother eagle quivered in anticipation that each would learn to fly. *"Why does the thrill of soaring have to begin with the fear of falling?"* she says. But she knew that until her "children" discovered their wings, there was no purpose for their lives. Until they learned how to soar, they would fail to understand the privilege it was to have been born an eagle. So she pushed them.

And they flew.

"Be it someone else who serves as our mother eagle pushing us from the nest, or simply the result of our own doing, most all of us get an opportunity to test the wind beneath our wings," I said. "In our day-to-day living, we may experience a gentle nudge (such as a traffic ticket) or a parting of the ways with a loved one (such as a divorce) that gets us to make a positive change. At other times, it's more than persuasion; we find ourselves at an important crossroad and are pushed, sometimes shoved, into making change. Either way, the task remains the same: when falling, learn to fly. Have any of you had such an experience?" I asked.

"That's exactly what happened to me," a young man by the name of Charles volunteered, "although I wouldn't say that I was 'persuaded' as much as *thrown* out of my nest."

"How so?" I asked, encouraging him to explain.

"Well," he said laughing nervously, "my flying had to do with rallying for my life. I was aspiring to be made a partner in my firm. Trouble was, in working toward becoming a partner, I was putting in grueling hours, days, nights, weekends. Everything else in my life became secondary, including my own health."

At the age of 36, a heart attack became Charles' "persuasion" to learn to fly.

"Lying in the hospital, certain that I was dying, I finally had a moment of clarity," he said in a somber tone. "My body was giving me a wake-up call. It was time to put some balance back into my life, or I wasn't going to have a life at all."

Clarity, of course, isn't enough. Action is required. "What did you learn 'in flight' so to speak?" I inquired.

"That I *had* to change—or else I wasn't going to live much longer. My 65-hour work schedule had become an addiction; I literally had to force myself to cut back to somewhat normal hours. I had to replace bad habits with healthy ones. Doing things like strictly adhering to an exercise and diet program was downright difficult, but my life depended on it. The bottom line is that if it hadn't been for the heart attack, I would have never made these health-based changes. I'd still be a stressed-out maniac, missing out on the valuable time I now spend with my wife and two sons—that is, if I was even still alive."

"Any surprises along the way?" I asked.

"You know, there was one real big surprise," he said thoughtfully. "Actually it was more like a rude awakening. I realized that even though others care about you, life is more of a solo trip than I care to believe. That's not to say that others—like the mother eagle—won't fret over whether or not we learn how to fly in the process. We are not alone in that regard; others *will* empathize with the task in front of us and, in one way or another, show support, maybe even coaching us as to what they think is best for us as we begin to falter. My wife and children love me and were supportive of me in every way. But I discovered that the earthly free-fall is an *individual* journey, or as Eleanor Roosevelt so aptly put it, 'Eventually one learns that it is neither your parents, spouse, or children who are responsible for your life, but rather, you, and you alone must take responsibility for how you lead your life.'"

Today Charles is a picture of a life in balance.

"I didn't know I was falling until I 'hit the bottom,'" said Josh, a 28-year-old. "My drug abuse had made a complete disaster of my life. It consumed me. My life went from bad to worse, and then, worse still. I was selling everything I owned, borrowing from everyone I could think of, writing bad checks—my whole world crashed in on me. Luckily, I got pulled over on a traffic offense one day and the police officer suspected (rightly so) I was high on something and took me to jail. That was just the beginning of my troubles. My wife said she would leave me—this time for good—if I didn't get help. I promised I would. My life had become a hell; I knew I needed help. It was the only way I could save my life."

"What did you learn?" I asked.

"Making this decision caused me to take a long hard look at my life. I was married, but only half-heartedly, which was about the same amount of enthusiasm I brought to life, as well. My life had no real meaning or direction."

"What are you doing differently now, as a result?" I asked.

"The best way to describe the attitude driving my choices now can be summed up by a line I heard in the movie, *The Shawshank Redemption:* 'I could either get busy living, or get busy dying.' I chose to get busy living."

Wanting him to expand on this, I probed, "How has that taken form for you?"

"I've decided to stop being so selfish and start working toward building a respectful relationship with my wife, and to work with young people who are substance abusers. Working with the kids gives me a whole new perspective —on the time I've lost and on the value of time. Life is shorter than we think. If I can help young people avoid the pitfalls I've fallen into, my life will have purpose after all. I leave liking who I am, feeling fulfilled. It's amazing, these feelings of finally finding myself only came after I was willing to lose myself in work for others."

"Any surprises along the way?" I asked.

"I had to practice rigorous honesty in all my affairs. When I didn't, I'd relapse and return to the hell of addiction, a place I never wish to be again," he said. "I had no clue what a day-by-day struggle it would be. This has caused me to get out of my denial, get honest, become authentic, live in the present. It's either that or death."

Josh has been drug-free for three years now.

"Sometimes it takes someone close to us, a coworker, a family member, a friend who cares enough to push us to fly even when we can't see the need ourselves," I began. "Can any of you relate?"

"That was me," Gena said. "I was a cheerleader in high school and homecoming queen. I got used to special treatment—and expected it to continue. After high school, I got a job and took my 'I-deserve-special-treatment' attitude with me. As a result, I lost three jobs in a row." Gena was on the verge of losing her fourth job when her boss gave her what Gena fondly refers to as a "kick in the butt."

"My boss, a dynamo woman manager whom I really respect, called me into her office one day and said, 'Gena, there are two kinds of people in this world. The ones who say they'll get the job done, and the ones who get it done. Take one week off and decide which kind you want to be.'"

Her boss's words helped Gena think about the role she wanted to play in her own life, and what she was willing to do in order to become a responsible person, to herself and others.

"What did you learn, Gena?" I asked.

"Basically, I had to come to terms with the fact I was no longer a kid, no longer a cheerleader, and start relating to others around me," she replied. "I had to learn to be helpful instead of simply demanding that others let me off the hook for being lazy, or accepting my low standards of performance. It was a helpful paradigm shift."

Investigating her growth from the experience, I asked, "Any surprises along the way?"

"There sure were," she said. "I stopped going out with only those men who catered to my every little whim. In the end I wouldn't respect these guys. I'm engaged now, and my fiancé appreciates that I can stand beside him as an equal and a real partner in our goals. Now I'm a helpmate, to my colleagues, my fiancé and to others who are in the world with me."

Today Gena is the director of sales at the company.

"Just as the opportunity to start flying offers the baby eagle a new beginning, so it can for us humans, too," I said. "One thing is for sure, catching the wind and learning to fly can be insightful. As many of you discovered, with all the fear that change causes, it also has redeeming features, one of them being to heighten our capacity to love ourselves and others. These are by no means shallow achievements."

"That's a fact!" Charles agreed. "Forced flight makes a lasting impression—not like the impression of snow angels, left to melt with the flakes and drifts they were formed in. These impressions are as lasting as a handprint left to harden in concrete."

"I would describe it in even stronger terms," Josh interjected. "I'd say the impression is forceful and direct, not like the mark left behind when a swung mallet misses and mars the surrounding finish, but rather, the impressions that were formed when carefully detonated sticks of dynamite shaped the faces of Mount Rushmore!"

Our learning to fly can be triggered by one of life's many crossroads: finding love or losing it, being hired or fired, the birth of a child, the death of a loved one, or something else entirely that gets our attention and causes us to re-evaluate our needs. Whatever the cause, this change in venue can be an important catalyst in keeping us from nodding off, alerting us to the fact that we are, in reality, starting a descent, spiraling downward. Such notice can prove useful: *We must get our wings flapping in order to save ourselves from a crash landing.*

One thing is for sure: there are lots of "flights" going on around us!

What can we learn from those who learn how "to fly" during the process of "a fall"? Like the baby eagle, each of us makes our own flight path, no two are identical; we each face our own assortment of pitfalls, grapple with hardships, trouble and calamity; we sacrifice, struggle, carry on—sometimes alone, many times weary and discouraged. And yet, we all travel through life together.

And so we share our thoughts, exchanging news of our journey. For what end? Can we heighten our consciousness—will we learn to be more aware—and take a big first step? Or, can we learn that we have a choice in the matter—not so much in falling (who can foresee the future?), but in the style of the flight (will I face this hardship/obstacle/situation with grace or grudge)? Can we learn something about the form we'd like to use in our flight (to turn inward/seek privacy or to turn outward/teach others)? Or, at a minimum—yet no less important—understand the *degree* of courage required (to face adversity with a spirit of determination to overcome, or resolutely give in and give up)?

If the challenge sometimes seems too great, we can take heart. We are not alone. Even an eagle needs a push.